PREPARING FOR PRACTICE

ASPEN COURSEBOOK SERIES

PREPARING FOR PRACTICE

Legal Analysis and Writing in Law School's First Year

AMY VORENBERG

University of New Hampshire School of Law

Wolters Kluwer

Law & Business

Copyright © 2015 CCH Incorporated.

Published by Wolters Kluwer Law & Business in New York.

Wolters Kluwer Law & Business serves customers worldwide with CCH, Aspen Publishers, and Kluwer Law International products. (www.wolterskluwerlb.com)

To contact Customer Service, e-mail customer.service@wolterskluwer.com, call 1-800-234-1660, fax 1-800-901-9075, or mail correspondence to:

Wolters Kluwer Law & Business
Attn: Order Department
PO Box 990
Frederick, MD 21705

Design and composition by Keithley & Associates, Inc.

Printed in the United States of America.

1 2 3 4 5 6 7 8 9 0

ISBN 978-1-4548-3616-2

Library of Congress Cataloging-in-Publication Data

Vorenberg, Amy, author.
  Preparing for practice : legal analysis and writing in law school's first year / Amy Vorenberg. — 1st Edition.
    pages cm
  Includes bibliographical references and index.
  ISBN 978-1-4548-3616-2 (alk. paper)
1. Legal composition. 2. Legal research—United States. I. Title.

  KF250.V67 2014
  808.06'634--dc23

                                        2014022985

About Wolters Kluwer Law & Business

Wolters Kluwer Law & Business is a leading global provider of intelligent information and digital solutions for legal and business professionals in key specialty areas, and respected educational resources for professors and law students. Wolters Kluwer Law & Business connects legal and business professionals as well as those in the education market with timely, specialized authoritative content and information-enabled solutions to support success through productivity, accuracy and mobility.

Serving customers worldwide, Wolters Kluwer Law & Business products include those under the Aspen Publishers, CCH, Kluwer Law International, Loislaw, Best Case, ftwilliam.com and MediRegs family of products.

CCH products have been a trusted resource since 1913, and are highly regarded resources for legal, securities, antitrust and trade regulation, government contracting, banking, pension, payroll, employment and labor, and healthcare reimbursement and compliance professionals.

Aspen Publishers products provide essential information to attorneys, business professionals and law students. Written by preeminent authorities, the product line offers analytical and practical information in a range of specialty practice areas from securities law and intellectual property to mergers and acquisitions and pension/benefits. Aspen's trusted legal education resources provide professors and students with high-quality, up-to-date and effective resources for successful instruction and study in all areas of the law.

Kluwer Law International products provide the global business community with reliable international legal information in English. Legal practitioners, corporate counsel and business executives around the world rely on Kluwer Law journals, looseleafs, books, and electronic products for comprehensive information in many areas of international legal practice.

Loislaw is a comprehensive online legal research product providing legal content to law firm practitioners of various specializations. Loislaw provides attorneys with the ability to quickly and efficiently find the necessary legal information they need, when and where they need it, by facilitating access to primary law as well as state-specific law, records, forms and treatises.

ftwilliam.com offers employee benefits professionals the highest quality plan documents (retirement, welfare and non-qualified) and government forms (5500/PBGC, 1099 and IRS) software at highly competitive prices.

MediRegs products provide integrated health care compliance content and software solutions for professionals in healthcare, higher education and life sciences, including professionals in accounting, law and consulting.

Wolters Kluwer Law & Business, a division of Wolters Kluwer, is headquartered in New York. Wolters Kluwer is a market-leading global information services company focused on professionals.

This book is dedicated to my students—
past, present, and future.

About the Author

Professor Amy Vorenberg has been teaching Legal Writing for over 16 years and is currently the Director of Legal Writing at the University of New Hampshire School of Law. She has published numerous articles in the field and presented frequently at academic conferences. She is a current board member of the Association of Legal Writing Directors.

Prior to her academic career, Ms. Vorenberg spent a decade in practice as an Assistant District Attorney in Manhattan, Assistant Attorney General in New Hampshire, and founding director of the NH Criminal Practice Clinic, a collaboration between the New Hampshire Public Defender's office and University of NH School of Law. She also served for ten years on the New Hampshire Adult Parole Board.

Other academic areas of expertise include Criminal and Juvenile Law.

Summary of Contents

Table of Contents

Acknowledgments

I am grateful to so many people who helped me with this book. My research assistants, Christian Ansah and Lindsay Whitelaw, not only helped with many of the sections, they also "vetted" the book by providing the student's perspective that was vital to the book's mission. Many colleagues and friends read drafts, edited, supported, or encouraged the project. In particular, Professors Risa Evans, Jessica Durkis-Stokes, Kimberly Kirkland, Erin Corcoran, Sue Zago, Calvin Massey, Michael Vorenberg, Melissa Greipp, and Sam and Kate Alberts read drafts and provided invaluable feedback. My assistant, Deborah Paige, kept me from pulling my hair out on more than one occasion. I have been well supported by the University of New Hampshire School of Law's administration. Kate Spoto, a former colleague and current practitioner, read a draft and gave me critical advice from the lawyer's perspective.

The crew at Wolters Kluwer have been wonderful. My gratitude to Christine Hannan, Carol McGeehan, Dana Wilson, and Sylvia Rebert, project manager, for Progressive Publishing Alternatives. To my family, Jill Alberts, Eliza Vorenberg, Roger Wellington, Nathan and Gabriel Maggiotto, and Kathryn Coughlin, you have been patient, supportive, and encouraging. And finally, to my fellow "writer" friends, Meg Cadoux Hirshberg and Lindley Shutz, if it were not for your initial push to put me onto this project, I would never have done it.

PREPARING FOR PRACTICE

PART I

LEGAL WRITING
Learning a New Language

CHAPTER 1

Introduction

A. WE'RE NOT IN KANSAS ANYMORE

You have arrived at law school with solid writing skills. After all, you would not be here without them. Legal writing, however, requires some unique skills. In many ways, learning legal writing is more like learning a new language. It is important to remember this because there will be times when you will say to yourself: "I thought I was a good writer. Why is this so much harder than my undergraduate research papers?" When these moments hit, remind yourself that legal writing is a genre you are not yet accustomed to.

First, in legal writing, less is more. Good legal writing means getting to the point quickly. This usually means that you start with your conclusion, so your reader understands where he or she is headed, and that you use short sentences and manageable paragraphs so the reader moves easily through your writing. If you were a political science major, or a student of humanities, this style may seem backward to you. Legal writing is focused on the reader, whereas academic writing is a product that reflects self-discovery. In legal writing, you are always asked to put yourself in the place of the reader.

Second, in many law practices, time is money. Written communication must therefore be done in the most expedient manner possible. Whether you are writing a letter or e-mail to a client, a colleague in your office, or an opposing counsel, you will likely be mindful that the time you spend researching and writing will cost the client money. The challenge is never sacrificing quality and accuracy for expedience.

Third, long gone are the days of "heretofore" and the "party-of-the-first-part." Effective legal writing is constructed with an attention to plain English. Writing like a lawyer means using language and structure that a client can understand. Colleagues and judges may understand the legal lingo better than a client, but they do not have the time or the patience to decipher complex words and dense paragraphs.

Finally, and perhaps most importantly, legal writing is a bit of a mischaracterization. You are actually learning how to analyze law and communicate about it effectively. That means that even before you learn how to write effectively, you must study and understand the law. Your legal writing class is about analyzing as much as about writing.

Consider yourself a student of a new language, a new way of communicating. Do not despair if your excellence in writing before law school does not seem to translate automatically into excellence in your first semester of law school. Be patient and you will soon see that, with guidance, the skills you have are indeed transferable to legal writing.

B. YOUR LEGAL WRITING CLASS

You will probably notice that your legal writing class doesn't look like your other first-year classes. Your legal writing class will be smaller. The book will be different, as it will likely be shorter and organized more like a reference book or textbook as opposed to a case book. The syllabus may look different. You will notice that you have more assignments due and that the course information for the class contains requisites for formatting, rubrics, or professionalism guidelines.

Remember, the first-year legal writing class is the first time you will get to act like a lawyer. In legal writing you learn law in the context of a hypothetical client's problem. You will communicate your analysis of the problem and solution in written documents. If you were in medical school this class would be the first "clinical" course, where you learn the basics of assessing a patient by interviewing and examining a mock patient.

You will also receive a lot of feedback from your professor. Perhaps for the first time in your life, you will receive detailed input about analysis, organization, grammar, and style. At first, this may come as a bit of a shock, but this is where you learn to transfer those solid writing skills you brought to law school into masterful legal writing. You would not be human if you did not wince a little (or a lot) when you receive copious feedback. Keep in mind that the feedback given is not personal; its only purpose is to help you become an effective lawyer. You and your professor share the exact same goal—that you succeed as a legal writer.

You could be in a legal office as early as next summer. It is better to make mistakes now and work through them with your professor than to make them when you are in the "real" world. Being open to critique and willing to work with your professor as a team will help you get the most out of your legal writing class.

C. CITATION? I HAVE TO LEARN THAT TOO?

You will notice that the cases you read for your other first-year classes rely on many kinds of authority, including other cases, statutes, and secondary sources, like the Restatement of Torts. Judges and lawyers use a uniform system of legal citation so that readers can easily find the authorities relied upon in documents. The citation system is governed by very particular rules. The *Bluebook* or the *ALWD Citation Manual* are the books you will use as references for citing accurately. You will likely use these books during and after law school, so hold on to them!

When you refer to cases, statutes, or other authorities in your legal writing, you will use the same type of uniform system and you will also have the *Bluebook* or the *ALWD Citation Manual* as your references. At first, the citation rules will seem mysterious and very persnickety. With practice, you will get used to the rules, become adept at learning how to cite, and the endeavor will become second nature to you. Again, be patient.

D. WHAT DO I NEED TO DO TO SUCCEED AT LEGAL WRITING?

The phrase legal writing professors hear over and over again during the first weeks of the semester is, "I can't believe how much time it takes to write a short memo!" Thus, the number one piece of advice is: Don't underestimate the time it takes to do the assignment. While waiting until the last minute may have worked in undergraduate school, it is unlikely to work in law school. Even a short, three-page assignment can take longer than you think it will.

The way to succeed in legal writing is as follows:

- Start early—plan ahead.
- Read the directions—know what is being asked.
- Meet with your professor and your teaching assistant.
- Learn to *study* (not just read) the law.
- Revise.
- Revise.
- Revise again.

Because learning about legal writing is like learning a new language, it will help if you are willing to make mistakes and learn from them. Becoming an effective legal analyst and writer is a **recursive** process. With each new assignment, you will have a chance to practice a skill you have already tried and learn new ones. Stay open to retrying, rethinking, and revising!

E. HOW THIS TEXTBOOK IS ORGANIZED

After this introduction and the first five chapters, this textbook has three case files. A case file contains the information you will need to solve the client's problem. The assigning memorandum and accompanying documents mirror the kind of information you are likely to be given in practice. With each case file, you will learn new skills and practice old ones. This book is set up to review acquired skills and introduce new ones as the book progresses into more complex legal problems.

The case files are meant to look like what you would work on in practice. They are also similar to the Multi-State Performance Test (MPT). The MPT is the bar exam testing format used by most states. A typical MPT includes a file and a library. The file consists of source documents containing all the facts of the case. The specific assignment is described in a memorandum from a supervising attorney. The file might also include transcripts of interviews, depositions, hearings or trials, pleadings, correspondence, client documents, contracts, newspaper articles, medical records, police reports, or lawyer's notes. The library includes the legal authorities, such as cases or statutes. The case files here look similar (though not identical) to the file and library contained in an MPT.

CHAPTER 2

How (and Why) Do Lawyers Communicate?

Lawyers do a lot of writing in many different forms. This chapter will give some examples of the common forms of legal writing. The remaining chapters will teach you how to do them.

A. WRITING TO EXPLAIN: THE PREDICTIVE ANALYSIS

Imagine that you have completed your first year of law school. You have an internship or a paid job with a firm, a government agency, a nonprofit organization, or a corporation. One of your new colleagues, perhaps your supervisor, asks you to find out the answer to a legal question that pertains to a client's case. She asks you to draft "something" that sets out the law on the particular question and also how the law might affect the client's situation.

The reason she is asking you to draft this information is likely because she is either deciding whether to pursue the client's case on this issue, or she has decided to take the case but wants to know everything about the issue before she drafts the complaint or writes a brief. That is why this is an objective analysis. Your colleague wants to be educated about the issue, not persuaded to go one way or the other on the issue.

What do you do? Your colleague is asking you to give her an objective analysis of the law on a particular issue. She is looking for information that both supports and opposes the client's position. First, you read the client's file (or whatever documents your colleague has given you), then you research the issue. Once you have a good idea of what the law is, you draft an outline and a legal memorandum. She may have asked you to e-mail her the results of your research.

Whether it is in an e-mail or a memorandum, the task is the same and the format is the same. You will begin with a statement of the issue followed by a brief answer (or summary) that addresses the particular issue. You may include a statement of the facts of the client's case, then you write the discussion. This is where you explain the law and then apply the law to the client's problem.

Here is an example of when you may be asked to write a predictive legal analysis. Let's say you are working in a firm and your supervisor tells you that one of her clients, who she represents primarily on business matters, has been accused of shoplifting. It turns out that the client has had similar trouble before. The lawyer is preparing to take the case to trial and wants to know if evidence of the client's prior misdeeds will be relevant (and thus potentially admissible) in the client's trial. She asks that you research and advise her on whether the evidence is legally relevant under state law.

What follows is an example of the predictive analysis you might return to her:

MEMORANDUM

To: Attorney Supervisor
From: Student Lawyer
Date: September 15, 2012
Re: *State v. Albert*: Criminal Theft—Relevance of Albert's prior shoplifting, #CR23456

Issue

In Maureen Albert's trial for theft of a ham from a Hannaford Supermarket (*Hannaford*), is evidence of a prior incident relevant where in the prior case Albert removed a turkey from the same Hannaford without paying?

Brief Answer

Probably yes. Evidence of Albert's earlier shoplifting incident is probably relevant under New Hampshire Rule of Evidence 404(b). Admission of prior bad act evidence under Rule 404(b) requires that: (1) the evidence is relevant for a purpose other than showing the defendant's character, (2) there is clear proof that the defendant actually committed the prior act, and (3) the probative value of the evidence outweighs its prejudicial impact. As instructed, this memo addresses only the question of relevance. Albert has made her intent an issue by specifically claiming she removed the ham accidentally. The evidence of Albert's prior shoplifting is thus likely relevant to rebut her claim that she took the ham by accident.

Facts

In November 2011, three months before the current incident occurred, Maureen Albert left the Hannaford's in Concord, New Hampshire, without paying for a turkey that she had placed in the bottom of her cart. Albert returned the turkey, was warned about her behavior, and was not prosecuted.

In February 2012, Albert took a cart containing a spiral ham out of the same Hannaford's without paying for it. When a Hannaford's employee stopped her in the parking lot, Albert said that she left the store because she realized she had forgotten her wallet in her car. She stated that she did not intend to steal the ham and had removed it from the store accidentally.

The State has charged Albert with shoplifting for the second incident. In her trial, the State wants to introduce evidence of the turkey incident to prove that she intended to steal the ham.

Discussion

Albert's prior act involving the turkey is relevant for a purpose other than character because she raised the issue of intent, and the prior act is factually similar and close in time to the charged act. Evidence is relevant for a purpose other than character if it (1) has a direct bearing on an issue actually in dispute, and (2) a clear and logical connection exists between that act and the crime charged. *McGlew*, 658 A.2d at 1194. The trial court must make specific findings on each of these elements. *Id.*

1. Direct Bearing on Issue in Dispute

Evidence of a prior act is relevant to refute a defendant's claim that the crime was committed by accident. *Lesnick*, 677 A.2d at 690. For example, the court in *Lesnick* admitted evidence of a prior act because it was relevant to show the absence of an accident where the defendant claimed she had stabbed her husband in self-defense because she believed him to be an unknown intruder. *Id.* In contrast, where the defendant denied any involvement at all in the crime, the court excluded the evidence. *State v. Blackey*, 623 A.2d 1333, 1334 (N.H. 1993). It reasoned that the evidence was not relevant because, by denying the crime altogether, the defendant had not placed her intent or propensity at issue. Id. at 1334; *State v. Whittaker*, 642 A.2d 936, 938 (N.H. 1994).

Albert's prior act is likely relevant here because she claims she took the ham by accident. Like the defendant in *Lesnick*, who admitted the stabbing but claimed it was an accident, Albert made her intent an issue by claiming she took the ham unintentionally. Evidence of a prior similar act is relevant to disproving Albert's claim of accident. Because the evidence of the prior act is offered for a purpose other than Albert's character or propensity to steal meat, it is probably admissible.

2. Clear and Logical Connection

Next, the evidence probably meets the second prong of the relevancy analysis because a clear, logical connection exists between the charged act of stealing a ham and the prior act of taking a turkey. A clear, logical connection exists where the acts are factually similar, and the prior act is "not so remote in time as to eliminate the nexus" between the prior act and the crime charged. *McGlew*, 658 A.2d at 1194. The State must articulate a precise chain of reasoning between the prior act and the charged act without relying on inferences about the defendant's character, which are forbidden. *Id.* at 1195. For example, in *Lesnick*, a logical connection existed between the prior stabbing and the charged stabbing because the defendant committed each crime under similar emotional circumstances against the same victim using the same weapon. *Id.* The factual similarities between the two acts permitted the conclusion that the defendant intended the second act since two identical "accidents" within a few months were unlikely. *Id.*

Where two acts are significantly different, the court will not admit evidence of the first one to prove the defendant's intent in committing the second act. In *McGlew* the State failed to establish a nexus between a prior accusation of sexual molestation and the charged act of sexual assault because the prior act, which occurred six years earlier, involved a victim of a different age and gender and a different sex act. 658 A.2d at 1194. The factual differences between the two acts suggested that the defendant might have had differing intent during each. *See Id.* (noting that the prior act was not relevant, although intent was an element of the charge).

In Albert's case, the turkey and the ham were similar products removed from the same store, using the same method of removal—all facts that show that the second incident was not an accident. Like *Lesnick*, where the close factual similarity between the prior act and the charged act made the prior act relevant to the defendant's intent, here the virtually identical facts probably make Albert's prior act relevant to her subsequent taking of the turkey.

Moreover, the close time frame between Albert's two incidents further strengthens their connection. The closer the temporal proximity between two acts, the more likely a court is to find that the actor had the same intent at both times. *See Lesnick*, 677 A.2d at 690 (emphasizing the temporal proximity of the charged act and the prior act). In *Lesnick*, the prior act was relevant because it occurred only two months before the charged crime, whereas in *McGlew*, the prior crime was not admitted, in part, because it occurred six years earlier. 658 A.2d at 1194. Similar to Lesnick, who committed the two acts within two months, Albert committed the two acts within three months. Although a person may make one mistake, she is unlikely to make two identical mistakes within a few months. The short time between Albert's two acts supports their logical connection. Because the prior act demonstrates Albert's intent, the court probably will find that the evidence meets the relevancy requirement of the three-part test.

Albert's only argument in her favor likely relies on the underlying purpose of 404(b). She could argue that allowing the bad act evidence against her goes against the purpose behind 404(b) and its limitations. *Id*. at 1195 (holding purpose underlying rule 404(b) is to ensure that a defendant is tried on the merits of the case and not on character). However, the concern that a defendant not be convicted on the basis of character is met where, as here, there is a sufficient, specific purpose for its admission. By claiming that she mistakenly took the turkey, Albert has placed her own intent to commit theft at issue. The prosecutor would probably be successful in arguing that the purpose of the evidence is to refute that claim and not to demonstrate her bad character.

Notice that the memorandum is an informative document that explains and applies the law and predicts that the prior evidence will come in as evidence in a trial against the client. The memorandum also includes a short counter-analysis at the end. This tells the reader that you have considered the opposing arguments and legal analysis. It also gives the reader a full picture of the legal issue. Remember that the memorandum is supposed to be a thorough and accurate analysis so that your supervisor can decide the best course of action; therefore it is important that any weaknesses in the case be addressed. This information will be critical to your supervisor, who will use it to advise the client on whether to take a plea in the case or go to trial.

B. WRITING TO INTERPRET: WRITING ABOUT LAW (NOT RELATED TO A CLIENT'S FACTS)

Predictive legal writing can take other forms. For instance, you may be asked to interpret a statute or explain a new case that has just come down. A predictive memorandum could also be used to prepare for a settlement negotiation or a decision not to file a complaint. Or, you may be asked to explain a statute or legal principle. For example, imagine that the firm or business where you are working has several clients who are landlords. A new version of a tenant eviction process has just been enacted. You have been asked to interpret the steps necessary to evict a tenant under the statute.

Here is an example of what your response would look like:

MEMORANDUM

To: Supervisor
From: Student Lawyer
Date: August 2, 2012
Re: New Hampshire Eviction Process

Question:

What steps are required to initiate and carry out eviction proceedings for a tenant who has not paid rent?

Summary of Relevant Law:

The eviction process in NH is a multi-step process set out in N.H. Rev. Stat. Ann. §540 and District Court Rule 5. First, the landlord must make a demand for rent. If no rent is paid then the landlord can file a Notice to Quit. The tenant is entitled to a hearing to challenge the demand. At the hearing, if the landlord sustains a claim of unpaid rent, the judge can order the tenant to pay back rent and a writ of possession that authorizes a sheriff to remove the tenant from the premises.

Steps to Evict a Tenant:

1. Demand for Rent

First, the landlord must make a demand for rent from the tenant. N.H. Rev. Stat. Ann. §540:3-4. The demand must state the amount owed and it must be served on the tenant personally or left at the residence. Either way, the landlord must show proof of the service by an attested copy of the demand and an affidavit that sets out that service was made. N.H. Rev. Stat. Ann. §540:5. The district court clerk's office has the forms needed; however, the landlord is not required to use the forms. N.H. Rev. Stat. Ann. §540:5.

2. Notice to Quit

The landlord must also provide the tenant with a written Notice to Quit (also called an "eviction notice"). N.H. Rev. Stat. Ann. §540:2(I). This can be done at the same time as the demand for rent. The Notice must be in writing and must state the specific reason for the eviction. N.H. Rev. Stat. Ann. §540:3(I-III)). When the reason for termination of tenancy is nonpayment of rent, 30 days' notice of eviction is sufficient. N.H. Rev. Stat. Ann. §540:3(II). The Notice to Quit must also inform the tenant that the tenant can avoid eviction by paying the past rent plus $15 in liquidated damages. N.H. Rev. Stat. Ann. §540:3(II), (III); 540:9.

3. Service of the Notice to Quit

The landlord can either serve the Notice to Quit personally with the tenant, or leave it at the tenant's residence. NH. Rev. Stat. Ann. §540: 5. Like the rule for the demand of rent, the landlord must show proof of the service by an attested copy of the Notice and an affidavit that sets out that service was made. The district court clerk's office has the forms needed. The landlord is not required to use the forms so long as all the information is on the notice. N.H. Rev. Stat. Ann. §540:5.

4. Writ of Summons

If the tenant has not complied with the demand for rent or the Notice to Quit, the landlord can go to the district court clerk's office and ask that the court issue a Writ of Summons. N.H. Rev. Stat. Ann. §540:13. Once the Writ is issued, a sheriff will serve the Writ and the tenant will have seven days to either leave the premises or request a hearing by filing an appearance at the district court. N.H. Rev. Stat. Ann. §540:13(II)(d)(1).

5. The Court Hearing

If the tenant requests a hearing, the court will schedule one within ten days after the date of the tenant's appearance is filed. N.H. Rev. Stat. Ann. §540:13(V). Both the tenant and the landlord are entitled to discovery prior to the hearing pursuant to N.H. Dist. Ct. R. 5.6. N.H. Rev. Stat. Ann. §540:13 (IV). At the hearing, the landlord would present the case for the unpaid rent and show proof of the demand and Notice to Quit. The tenant is allowed to present evidence in defense. N.H. Rev. Stat. Ann. §540:13(III). The court will decide the matter and can award the landlord the unpaid rent up to $1,500.

If the tenant does not file an appearance, the court will send a notice of default to the tenant within three days of issuing a Writ of Possession. N.H. Rev. Stat. Ann. §540:14(I). Once the Writ of Possession is issued the sheriff is authorized to remove the tenant from the premises.

Notice that this memorandum is purely about law. There is no application of the law to a client's problem.

Predictive writing is typically done "in house," meaning that it is done for internal use. In other words, it is done within a law office or by a clerk in a judge's chambers. Because this type of legal writing is done to inform and educate and not to persuade, there is little likelihood of writing an objective analysis in a brief for a court. That is where persuasive legal writing comes in.

C. WRITING TO PERSUADE: THE PERSUASIVE MEMORANDUM OR BRIEF

Now imagine that you have completed your first year of law school and you are working in a state prosecutor's office. You are asked to draft a persuasive motion *in limine* arguing that the prior evidence regarding Albert's removal of the turkey from the supermarket should be admissible in a trial against her for the theft of the ham.

The format and content of persuasive legal writing is similar to objective writing. However, instead of informing the reader, the task is to *convince* the reader that whatever position you want the court to take is supported and thus should prevail. The tone (language) used will be slightly different. Notice in the example below how similar the structure and content of the memorandum is to the predictive memorandum.

MERRIMACK, SS.   SEPTEMBER TERM 2013
                              SUPERIOR COURT

State of New Hampshire
v.
Maureen Albert
No. 000-2013-CV-0000

STATE'S MOTION *IN LIMINE* TO ADMIT EVIDENCE OF OTHER BAD ACTS

NOW COMES the State of New Hampshire, by and through its attorney, Leslie Witman of the Office of the State Prosecutor, and hereby seeks an order from this Court admitting evidence to trial regarding Defendant Maureen Albert's (hereinafter "Albert" or "Defendant") prior bad act of shoplifting a turkey from a Hannaford Supermarket.

INTRODUCTION

Defendant's prior bad act of shoplifting is admissible under New Hampshire Rule of Evidence 404(b) because it is relevant to show Defendant's intent, not mere character evidence; there is clear proof that the Defendant actually committed the act; and the probative value of the evidence outweighs any prejudicial impact on a jury. As previously stipulated, this motion addresses only the first question of relevance.

Defendant is currently charged with theft of a ham from a Hannaford Supermarket in Concord, New Hampshire in February 2012, just three months after a similar incident in which Defendant shoplifted a turkey from the same store. By claiming that she did not intend to steal the ham for which she is currently charged, Defendant put her own intent at issue. As such, Defendant's similar prior act is relevant to her state of mind at the time of the second shoplifting incident and ought to be admissible to rebut her claim that she stole the meat by mere accident.

In further support of its motion to admit this evidence at trial, the State says as follows:

BACKGROUND

Ms. Maureen Albert removed a turkey placed in the bottom of her shopping cart without paying from the Hannaford's Supermarket in Concord, New Hampshire in November 2011. Albert returned the turkey after being confronted, was warned about her behavior, and was not prosecuted. Just three months later, in February 2012, Albert shoplifted a spiral ham using a shopping cart from the same store. When confronted by an employee in the parking lot, Albert stated that she left the store because she had forgotten her wallet in her car. She brought her state of mind into issue even further by also stating that she did not intend to steal the ham and had removed it from the store accidentally. The State has now charged Albert with shoplifting for the second offense.

ARGUMENT

Ms. Maureen Albert's prior act of taking a turkey from the Concord, New Hampshire Hannaford's without paying is relevant to prove that she intended to shoplift the ham for which she is currently charged from the same store. When evidence has a direct bearing on an issue actually in dispute, and a clear and logical connection exists between that act and the crime charge, then the evidence is relevant for a purpose other than character. *McGlew*, 658 A.2d 1191, 1194. Albert's prior act is relevant to refute her claim that she took the ham accidentally. In addition, the prior act is factually similar and close in time because she removed meat without paying twice in three months from the same store.

1. Direct Bearing on Issue in Dispute

Albert's prior act of taking a turkey is relevant to refute her claim that shoplifting the ham was by accident. Generally, evidence of a prior act is relevant to refute a defendant's claim that the crime was committed by accident. *Lesnick*, 677 A.2d 686, 690 (N.H. 1996). For example, in *Lesnick*, where the defendant claimed she stabbed her husband in self-defense because she believed him to be an unknown intruder, the court admitted evidence of a prior act because it was relevant to show that absence of an accident. *Id*. In contrast, when a defendant denies any involvement in a crime, prior act evidence is excluded. *State v. Blackey*, 623 A.2d 1333, 1334 (N.H. 1993). By denying the crime altogether, the defendant in *Blackey* had not placed her intent or propensity at issue, so the prior act evidence was not relevant and the court excluded it. *Id*.

Albert's prior act is relevant because she claimed that she took the ham by accident. Similar to the defendant in *Lesnick*, who admitted to stabbing her husband but claimed it was by accident, Albert made her intent an issue by claiming she took the ham unintentionally when returning to her car. Evidence of her prior similar act is relevant to rebut Albert's claim of taking the ham by accident. Because the evidence of the prior removal of meat is not offered to show Albert's character or propensity, but rather to rebut her claim of mere mistake, it is admissible.

2. Clear and Logical Connection

Albert's prior act is also relevant because a clear, logical connection exists between the charged act of shoplifting a ham and the prior act of taking a turkey from the same store within three months of each other. Where the acts are factually similar, and the prior act is "not so remote in time as to eliminate the nexus" between the prior act and the crime charged, then a clear, logical connection exists. *McGlew*, 658 A.2d at 1194. Where a precise chain of reasoning between the prior act and the charged act exists, the prior evidence is admissible. *Id*. at 1195. In *Lesnick*, a logical connection existed between the prior stabbing and the charged stabbing because the defendant committed each crime under similar emotional circumstances against the same victim using the same weapon. *Id*. The factual similarities between the two acts concluded that the defendant intended the second act since two identical "accidents" within a few months of each other were unlikely. *Id*.

Albert's prior act and current charge are so significantly similar that a clear and logical nexus connects the two events. In *McGlew*, where a prior accusation of sexual molestation and the charged act of sexual assault, which occurred six years later, involved a different victim of different age and gender and a different sex act, the prior charge was inadmissible because there was not a sufficient nexus between the two acts. 658 A.2d at 1194. The factual differences could not permit the conclusion that the defendant had the same intent during each act and therefore the prior act was inadmissible. *Id*.

The virtually identical facts of Albert's two acts permit the conclusion that she intended the second act since two identical "accidents" within such a short time frame is unlikely. The turkey and ham were similar products removed from the same store, using the same method of removal—suggesting that the second shoplifting incident was intentional. Similar to the facts in *Lesnick*, where the close similarity of the two acts rendered the prior act relevant to the defendant's intent in stabbing her husband, here the virtually identical circumstances and facts permit the conclusion that Albert's prior act is also relevant to her intent to steal the ham.

In addition to the factual similarities of Albert's two acts, the time frame between the two shoplifting incidents further indicates that her intent was to steal the ham. When two acts are close in proximity, the more likely an actor had the same intent at both times. *See Lesnick*, 677 A.2d at 690 (emphasizing the temporal proximity of the charged act and the prior act). In *Lesnick*, the prior act was relevant because it occurred only two months before the charged crime, whereas in *McGlew*, the prior act committed six years earlier was not admitted. 677 A.2d at 690; 658 A.2d at 1194. Albert's prior removal of a ham and subsequent shoplifting of a turkey just three months later is similar to Lesnick, who committed the two acts within two months. Although a person may make one mistake, she is unlikely to make two nearly identical mistakes within such a short time. The close proximity in time between Albert's two acts further supports their logical connection and renders her prior act of shoplifting relevant. Because the prior act demonstrates Albert's intent, and is not mere character or propensity evidence, it is relevant to the current charge.

Albert's argument that allowing the bad act evidence against her goes against the purpose behind 404(b) and its limitations is without merit. The concern that a defendant not be convicted on the basis of character is met where, as here, there is a sufficient, specific purpose for its admission. By claiming that she mistakenly took the turkey, Albert has placed her own intent to commit theft at issue. Thus, the purpose of the evidence is to refute Albert's claim of accident, and not to demonstrate her bad character.

WHEREFORE the State of New Hampshire respectfully requests that this Honorable Court:
  A. Find that evidence of Defendant's prior act of taking a turkey from the Concord, New Hampshire Hannaford's in November 2011 is admissible at Albert's trial; and
  B. Grant such other and further relief as this Court deems just and proper.

Respectfully submitted,
THE STATE OF NEW HAMPSHIRE
By its attorney,
By: /s/ Leslie Witman
Leslie Witman
NH Bar # 000
Assistant County Attorney
County Prosecutors Bureau
3 Main Street
Concord, NH 03301

Date: September 22, 2013

CERTIFICATE OF SERVICE

I hereby certify on this 22nd day of September 2013, copies of the foregoing Motion *In Limine* were sent by e-mail to Maureen Albert and her counsel.

/s/ Leslie Witman, Esq
Leslie Witman, Esq

D. WRITING TO A CLIENT: COMMUNICATING TO A LAYPERSON

Communicating with clients makes up a lot of what lawyers do. Typically, lawyers write to clients to keep them updated and to explain to them the legal, practical, and procedural ramifications of their cases. Client letters (which are often done in e-mails) can also memorialize decisions that clients have made, such as to settle a case or proceed to court. In addition, client letters may address whether a client wants to agree to a contract term.

While some clients will be lawyers, most legal correspondence is between a lawyer and a non-lawyer. This book, and most legal writing instruction, will demand that you always write in plain English. However, the need for clarity is especially critical when writing to a client.

Here is an example of a client letter that Albert's lawyer might send her regarding whether she should plead guilty to a reduced sentence and avoid a trial. Notice the absence of specific references to cases.

Maureen Albert
3 Pike Street
Concord, New Hampshire

Re: Shoplifting case

Dear Ms. Albert:

As requested, I am writing to give you my opinion on whether you should accept the prosecutor's offer of a misdemeanor plea and a probationary sentence. As you and I discussed, the key question is whether your prior incident at the same Hannaford will come into the trial as evidence. If the judge allows the evidence, the likelihood of a not guilty verdict diminishes. This letter will address why the prior incident will likely be allowed into evidence.

Explanation of Relevant Law

As I explained to you at our meeting, evidence of prior similar activity is allowed to come into a trial under certain limited circumstances. The prior incident must be relevant for a purpose other than just to show character. In other words, the prior incident must have a direct bearing on the current case and there must be a clear, logical connection between the prior incident and the current case. Thus, the judge can allow prior evidence of similar conduct if the prosecutor can prove that the evidence is relevant and that there is a logical reason to do so.

Your Case

The prosecutor will argue that the incident involving the ham should be allowed at your trial because it involves very similar conduct and it shows that you didn't take the turkey by accident. In your trial, the prosecutor will have to prove that you had an intent to steal the turkey. She will argue that, by claiming that the turkey removal was an accident, you have put your intent at issue, which, she will say, opens the door for her to put in evidence of the ham incident. She will argue that your claim of accident can be refuted because you did a similar act recently. In addition, she will argue that the two scenarios are so similar and close in time that you could not have removed the turkey by accident.

I think that there is a good chance that the judge will allow evidence of your prior incident to come into the trial. Because the acts are so similar and close in time, the judge will probably find that the jury can use the evidence as proof that you did not take the turkey by accident. We will argue that this evidence would unfairly prejudice the jury against you and there is law we can use to support this argument. However, my belief is that the judge will not rule in our favor.

Conclusion and Next Steps

The prosecutor has offered one year of probation in exchange for your guilty plea to the theft. Whether to accept this offer is entirely up to you. If you decide to reject the offer, I will do my best to represent you at trial. It can be hard to predict what a jury will do. However, given the likelihood that the judge will allow the prior incident to come into evidence, I think it will be difficult, though not impossible, to get a not guilty verdict. If you were to go to trial, the judge could give you a longer probationary sentence, deferred jail time, or actual jail time (though I think this is unlikely). Given what you have told me about your need to care for your family and your desire to put this incident behind you, I would advise that you accept the prosecutor's offer. I am happy to discuss this further. I know it is a big decision and you want to feel as though you are making the right choice for you.

Please call my office and set up a time to go over this information and any questions you have.

Sincerely,

Lawyer

There are, of course, many other kinds of writing that you will do: drafting legislation, making notes to a file, writing judicial opinions (if you are a judicial law clerk or become a judge), writing contracts and legal documents, and perhaps writing scholarly pieces. And in law school (and on the bar exam), you will be writing exam answers. The skills you learn in your legal writing class will help you be an effective writer in all of these situations.

CHAPTER 3

Where Does the Law We Use Come From?

Learning to write effectively as a lawyer means you will need to be a good and careful analyzer of the law. In the United States, law comes from many sources and this chapter will review those sources.

You will notice that in your other courses, like Torts and Civil Procedure, many of the cases you read are appellate opinions. Appellate opinions come from courts that review the decisions of lower courts and administrative bodies. Appellate opinions make good vehicles for learning law because they often summarize and apply important legal concepts. You will also read cases from trial level courts. Typically, these cases address pretrial issues, such as decisions on motions on evidentiary issues and motions to dismiss. Often a case will settle after a court has ruled on a pretrial motion.

Keep in mind that the opinions you read are often the last chapter of a legal issue that began with a client's problem. The case probably started where most cases start: when a client goes to see a lawyer for help. Clients come in all shapes and sizes, including individuals, corporations, state agencies, or nonprofit organizations. When a client comes to a lawyer, it is typically to solve a problem or answer a question. The first step for the lawyer is to figure out what laws will determine the solutions or answers.

Let's say that a 60-year-old woman comes to a lawyer because she has been fired and she thinks her employer was wrong. She suspects she is being discriminated against on the basis of her age and has evidence to support her suspicion. How do you figure out whether it was legally wrong? You will have to learn if there are state or federal statutes or regulations that govern employment matters. Perhaps there are court opinions either from the state or federal courts. There might be regulations promulgated by state or federal agencies that prohibit termination on the basis of age. In other words, understanding what makes up our system of rules and laws is critical to being a lawyer.

Most lawyers will end up specializing in one area of law. With experience, the statutes, cases, regulations, and practices in the area in which you specialize will become familiar. As a newcomer to the field, it will help you, no matter which area of practice you eventually choose, to understand the overall framework of our system of laws.

The U.S. Constitution is the highest law of the land. The Constitution establishes a power-sharing form of government between the national (federal) government and state governments, known as federalism. This is different from a centralized system of power, such as that practiced in France or the United Kingdom.

The Constitution enumerates the powers of the federal government and reserves the non-enumerated powers to the state governments. The states are supreme in matters reserved to them, although there is very little that is expressly reserved to states because their power begins only where valid federal authority ends. For those matters that are reserved to the states, such as establishing local governments or regulating intra-state commerce, each state is sovereign and eligible to make and interpret its own laws without any interference from other states and the federal government. As a result, each of the 50 states has its own constitution, statutes, and other forms of law.

Keep in mind that all provisions of the state constitution must comply with the U.S. Constitution and federal statutory law. For instance, a state constitution cannot deny an accused criminal the right to a jury trial because the U.S. Constitution would prohibit such a law. The Supremacy Clause of the U.S. Constitution provides that federal law is superior to state law.

What follows is a brief review in civics (for purposes of background and foundation) and a general summary of how the law is structured in the United States.

There are three branches of government in the United States: the legislative, the judiciary, and the executive. All three branches make law. Every state has the same structure with three branches that also make law.

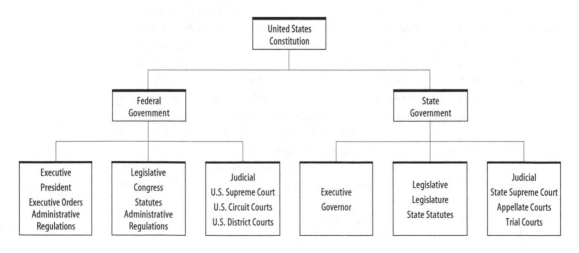

A. THE EXECUTIVE BRANCH

1. The Federal Executive

a. Federal Regulations

Because Congress cannot legislate with the detail necessary to implement all its laws, the executive branch creates administrative agencies that implement federal law (such as the U.S. Department of Agriculture). Congress often provides agencies the authority to promulgate rules and regulations that execute the federal law. These regulations, as well as proposed regulations, are recorded in the *Federal Register*, a daily publication that reports the daily activities of the executive branch. When these regulations are made final, they are codified in the *Code of Federal Regulations (CFR)*, a collection of all the regulations currently in force put in order of subject.

For example, in 1946 Congress passed the National School Lunch Program (NSLP), which reimburses schools for the cost of providing free and reduced lunch to its income-eligible students. In order to inform schools and the public about how the NSLP works, the U.S. Department of Agriculture (the agency created by the executive branch to make policy on farming, agriculture, and food), promulgated regulations that specified the program details. Here is an excerpt from a regulation:

> (i) *Requirements for lunch.* School lunches offered to children age 5 or older must meet, at a minimum, the meal requirements in paragraph (b) of this section. Schools must follow a food-based menu planning approach and produce enough food to offer each child the quantities specified in the meal pattern established in paragraph (c) of this section for each age/grade group served in the school. In addition, school lunches must meet the dietary specifications in paragraph (f) of this section. Schools offering lunches to children ages 1 to 4 and infants must meet the meal pattern requirements in paragraph (p) of this section. 7 CFR 210.10

b. Legislation Proposals

The executive branch proposes many of the bills that are considered by Congress. Similarly, a state's executive branch proposes bills that are considered by state legislators.

c. Executive Orders

Article II of the U.S. Constitution grants to the president certain broad powers, including the power to issue executive orders. These orders, also called presidential directives, are effectively laws, but they do not need to be approved by Congress. Executive orders can be challenged in court, and legal scholars argue about the extent of presidential power to issue orders. The orders are numbered and recorded in the *Federal Register* and the *CFR.*

2. The State Executive

a. Legislation Proposals

A state's executive branch can draft proposals for consideration by the state's legislature.

b. State Regulations

Similar to federal regulations, a state's executive branch creates administrative agencies pursuant to statutory authority (i.e., from the legislative branch). These agencies issue administrative regulations.

c. Executive Orders

State governors have the power to make executive orders. These orders are not laws and they do not require legislative approval, but they are binding.

B. THE LEGISLATIVE BRANCH

1. Federal Laws

The U.S. Constitution gives Congress (made up of the House and the Senate) enumerated powers to make laws. Article I of the Constitution specifies the matters on which Congress is allowed to legislate. Congress is not allowed to make laws relating to matters not listed in Article I. Current federal laws are organized by subject and put into the federal code (United States Code Annotated - U.S.C.A.).

2. State Laws

State constitutions give state legislatures the power to enact laws. If a state enacts a law relating to a matter reserved to the U.S. Congress by the Constitution and Congress passes a conflicting law, the state law will be preempted. Each state publishes its current laws in a code.

C. THE JUDICIAL BRANCH

1. Overview

The federal judicial branch includes the U.S. Supreme Court and lower federal courts. Every state has its own judicial branch that includes a state supreme court and inferior courts. Each system is responsible for deciding cases within its jurisdiction; the federal judiciary decides cases within the federal system and each state system decides cases within its state. The state and federal court systems operate parallel to one another, although the two systems can interact with one another; thus, the two systems are not completely independent.

Courts make law. They do this by upholding, interpreting, or striking down statutes that have been challenged, or by upholding or amending previous court decisions. Remember that a case usually begins in the lowest court (the trial court) and typically goes no further because it is either resolved or settled early. Generally, the decisions made by state trial court judges (called orders) are not published. They are written down and become a part of the court's case file. There are exceptions—with technology and online research services, some trial court orders do get published. Federal trial court opinions (which are longer than orders) are published.

Some cases are appealed to higher courts and it is in these decisions, which are recorded and published, that the courts make law. The appellate cases you read for your other courses all started with a client who had a problem. This case law makes up a large portion of the law that lawyers must use to help solve their clients' problems. Statutes make up the other portion of the law.

Legal cases fall into two main categories: civil and criminal. Civil cases are lawsuits to recover damages or to stop others from doing something. These are normally disputes among private individuals and businesses, though government institutions can also be party to civil actions. Conversely, criminal cases are lawsuits that seek punishment in the form of imprisonment or fine. In criminal cases, the government brings a lawsuit on behalf of the public against an individual who violated a criminal law. In a civil suit, the party bringing the lawsuit is the plaintiff and the party defending the lawsuit is the defendant. In a criminal suit, the accused is called the defendant and the party bringing the case is called the state, the government, or the commonwealth.

2. The Federal Court System

The federal courts are only permitted to hear limited types of cases. The Constitution specifies the types of cases the U.S. Supreme Court can hear. When Congress created the federal trial courts and intermediate courts, it passed laws defining what types of cases the lower federal courts could hear.

Generally, the federal courts hear cases that involve questions of federal law, including the U.S. Constitution, federal statutes, cases in which the United States is a party, and cases involving U.S. citizens and citizens of other countries. They also hear state law cases between citizens of different states; however, they must apply state law. Cases at federal courts begin at the trial court level, which is called the U.S. District Court. Unsatisfied parties can appeal the decision to the appellate court, known as circuit court, and finally to the court of last resort, the U.S. Supreme Court. Congress has also established other inferior courts in the federal court system, such as bankruptcy and tax courts.

a. U.S. District Courts

The U.S. District Court is the lowest level of federal courts. This is where a litigant's case will usually enter the court system. The issue may involve a prior decision of an agency (e.g., the IRS). This is the only level in the lawsuit where parties have the chance to present evidence to support their claims. Judges determine issues of law and the jury examines the evidence of the parties (facts) and how those facts apply to the law. Ninety-four U.S. district courts exist in the United States, and every state has at least one.

The kinds of cases heard in a U.S. District Court include criminal cases involving violation of federal laws (e.g., kidnapping, bank robbery, or drug trafficking), civil cases involving claims that a federal law has been violated (e.g., the Constitution or U.S. treaties), civil cases between parties of different states alleging violation of state law for amounts in excess of $75,000 (these are cases brought under "diversity jurisdiction"), and civil actions brought by or against the United States. The U.S. district court also hears appeals of certain federal agency decisions, such as Social Security Appeals Council decisions.

b. U.S. Circuit Courts of Appeals

The United States has 13 circuit courts. The federal circuit courts are appellate courts. The nation is divided geographically into 12 circuit boundaries, each with a circuit court. There is a 13th circuit which sits in Washington, D.C. A party dissatisfied with a district court ruling can appeal to the circuit court within his or her jurisdiction, except in criminal cases where the court finds the accused not guilty. There is no appeal of a not guilty verdict, and the case ends with the verdict. Generally, the circuit courts do not review the facts of the cases that have come before them. They accept the facts that have been found by either a jury or a judge. The circuit courts examine whether mistakes exist in the lower court's decision about what the law is and how it applies to the facts of a given case. Hence, no additional evidence is taken at this stage. Occasionally, a circuit court will review facts, but only if there has been a clearly erroneous decision with regard to the facts. The court normally sits in panels of three.

c. U.S. Supreme Court

The Supreme Court is the highest court of the land and is located in Washington, D.C. The Supreme Court is also an appellate court. Parties unsatisfied with a circuit court decision or a state supreme court decision (if it involves federal law—more on that later) can petition the U.S. Supreme Court through a "petition for a writ of certiorari" to hear their case. Not all cases get to the Supreme Court. The Court decides to hear a case when four justices agree on it. The Court is made up of nine justices and all of the justices sit in all cases before the Court.

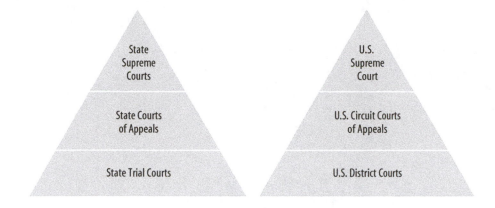

3. The State Court System

Like the federal system, most state courts have three levels of courts: a trial court where most lawsuits begin, an intermediate court, and the highest court. However, some states, including New Hampshire, Nevada, Montana, and Vermont, among others, have only two levels: a trial court and a supreme court.

a. Trial Courts

Almost all state courts have two kinds of trial courts: a court of limited jurisdiction that hears special cases (probate, family, juvenile, municipal, traffic matters, etc.) and a court that hears criminal and civil matters.

b. Intermediate Courts

Many, but not all, states have appellate courts between their trial courts and their highest court. Intermediate courts are normally based on districts or counties. Dissatisfied parties to a lawsuit in a trial court may appeal to an appropriate intermediate court. The intermediate courts of appeal generally deal with mistakes in the law and procedural errors made in the trial court. Occasionally, intermediate courts will review a lower court's findings of fact, but typically this occurs only when there is a clear error.

c. Highest State Court

Not all states call their highest courts "supreme courts." For instance, the highest courts in Maryland and New York are the court of appeals. Confusingly, New York calls its trial courts supreme courts. The highest courts of states without intermediate courts directly hear appeals from their trial courts. The highest state courts may have original jurisdiction in certain controversies. All cases in states end at this level, except in matters involving federal law, since the U.S. Supreme Court has the final word in matters of federal law. Most cases are never heard by the U.S. Supreme Court. Approximately 10,000 cases are submitted to the Court annually and only about 75 to 80 are accepted.

CHAPTER 4

How We Use the Law: Hierarchy of Law

Lawyers look for legal solutions to their clients' problems. The law or rules they look for depend on the facts of each client's case. Once a lawyer has identified the legal issue or issues that the client's problem fits into (e.g., age discrimination in employment; admission of a prior bad act in a criminal trial), the next step is to look for the law that will answer the problem. The law may come from constitutions, statutes, cases, regulations, or local ordinances referred to in Chapter 3.

There is a hierarchy of law: primary authority and secondary authority. Primary authority (the actual rules of law) carries more weight in resolving a legal issue than secondary authority (information about the law, such as law reviews or legal encyclopedias). The law you rely on to answer your client's problem will depend on several factors, such as what state you are in and whether the legal issue is addressed by federal or state law.

Primary authority can be either mandatory or persuasive. For example, if you are arguing a case in Nebraska, but one of the cases you are relying on is from Indiana, the Indiana case will be considered by the Nebraska court as primary authority (it contains actual rules), but it is not mandatory that the Nebraska court follow the case. This means that it will be persuasive, but not mandatory. In other words, some authority is decisive—you will have to follow it, and some is guiding—you can use it to shore up your position, but it isn't binding on the body deciding the legal question.

What follows is a summary of the precedential value that the different sources of law have. Keep in mind that understanding the sources and weight of law will become clearer when you are in the process of solving a client problem and you have a context for what you are researching.

A. PRIMARY SOURCES OF LAW

Primary sources of law represent actual rules of law and are promulgated by entities that are empowered to create law, such as courts and legislatures. Constitutions, statutes, regulations, and cases are primary authority. Other sources may include court rules, municipal charters, and ordinances. Primary authority may be mandatory or persuasive. Mandatory authority is binding within a jurisdiction, and hence, courts must follow it. Conversely, persuasive authority does not bind courts in a jurisdiction, but can influence a court's decision.

1. Constitutions

Constitutions are the highest laws of a land and, therefore, the most fundamental, authoritative sources of law. Typically, a state publishes its constitution in the beginning or the end of its statutory compilations. The U.S. Constitution is published in the United States Code (U.S.C.).

2. Statutes

State legislatures make statutes. Before laws become statutes, the legislature first enacts and publishes them as slip laws. Several slip laws are then compiled into session laws, which are later incorporated into statutory codes. The federal government has its own statutes. Federal statutes compilations include the United States Code (U.S.C.), United States Code Annotated (U.S.C.A.), and United States Code Service (U.S.C.S.).

3. Regulations

Regulations are agency-generated rules that have the force of law. Both federal and state agencies promulgate rules to implement and interpret certain statutory provisions. For example, the Family Educational Rights and Privacy Act of 1974 (FERPA) is a federal law designed to give parents or eligible students certain rights related to educational records. The U.S. Department of Education administers the laws and promulgates regulations to implement and enforce the law.

4. Judicial Opinions

Judicial opinions interpret statutes and regulations as well as prior cases. Thus, cases are next in the hierarchy authority after statutes and regulations. Because cases can be either mandatory or persuasive authority, prioritizing is important in citing them. The general rule is that a state's supreme court cases within a jurisdiction are binding on all lower courts within that jurisdiction. For instance, all federal circuit courts and federal district courts must follow a decision (precedent) set by the U.S. Supreme Court. State courts must follow the ruling of the highest court of their state. However, a decision by the highest court of a state is only persuasive authority in courts of other states.

5. Mandatory Versus Persuasive Authority

Mandatory law *must* be followed by a court. Persuasive law *may* be followed by a court. In a state with an intermediate (appeals) court, a decision by the appellate court is binding on lower (trial) courts, but can only be persuasive in a litigant's case before the state's supreme court. An intermediate appeals court opinion provides persuasive authority to other intermediate appeals courts if a state has multiple mid-level appeals courts (e.g., in New York, there are four Appellate Division Courts). Such intermediate courts' opinions can also be persuasive in other states as well. In the federal system, a decision by a circuit court is only binding on lower courts within that circuit. For example, a decision by the First Circuit Court of Appeals is only binding in the U.S. district courts of Maine, New Hampshire, Massachusetts, Puerto Rico, and Rhode Island. The opinions of one circuit court are persuasive authority to another circuit court and U.S. district courts under other circuits.

Decisions by state trial courts and U.S. district courts carry the least weight. A decision by a particular trial court or U.S. District Court in a jurisdiction is not binding on other trial courts in that jurisdiction. However, lower court opinions can be persuasive to other lower courts or even higher courts within its jurisdiction. This is especially true when a trial court has written an opinion that is exactly on point with an issue before another court. It is important to cite to the authorities within a given jurisdiction based on the level of the court in that jurisdiction.

Judicial decisions are collected in reporters. Each state publishes its decisions in the reporters. Some of the reporters include the *North Eastern Reporter* and the *North Western Reporter,* among others.

Quite often, lawyers and judges turn to another state's law—especially case law—if their own state has not addressed a particular legal issue that the other state has. Sometimes lawyers or judges who have a case in federal court will look to state case law if there is no federal case law on point (i.e., that is relevant to the case at hand). These situations all involve using persuasive authority rather than mandatory authority. The law used for support may be primary, but is not binding and may be very helpful in deciding the issue because another court or legal body has already addressed it.

For example, recall the case about the 60-year-old woman who comes to you because she believes she was fired because she is old, not because she is incompetent. Let's say that the state you are in has a state statute that prohibits discrimination based on age. That statute is primary authority that is also mandatory. Now, imagine that you are gathering research and you find cases from your state's highest court that interpret the language of the statute. Those cases are also mandatory authority. In addition, you realize that *another* state has a very similar antidiscrimination statute as well as some cases that interpret that state's statute. Because the cases are interpreting a statute that is very similar to your state statute, the cases have persuasive value. In other words, you can use the cases to shore up and support your position, but these cases have persuasive weight, not mandatory, binding weight.

The case that follows (*Diaz v. Krob*) is also an example where the parties and the court used other states' law to help decide an issue that had not yet been addressed in their own state. In the case, a woman was crossing a street when she stopped at the center median because the "Don't Walk" warning activated. A school bus driver stopped and motioned her to cross in front of the bus and the woman was struck and injured by a car. One issue in the case was whether the school bus driver had a duty to the woman whom he signaled (you will recognize the concept of "duty" from your torts class). Notice in the paragraph beginning with a "6" the court says, "The parties assert that the issue of whether a duty exists under the circumstances of this case is one of first impression in Illinois. The parties cite various out-of-state rulings in support of their respective positions." Because there are no similar cases in Illinois, the parties are using other states' case law (Michigan and New York) to persuade the court in Illinois to adopt their position. This is an example of primary authority (Michigan and New York case law) that is persuasive (i.e., it is not binding on the Illinois court).

264 Ill.App.3d 97
Appellate Court of Illinois,
Third District.

Janet L. DIAZ and Jaime Diaz, wife and husband, Plaintiffs-Appellants,
v.
Grace KROB and Joliet Township High School District #204, Defendants-Appellees.
No. 3-93-0852. | June 30, 1994.

Pedestrian whom automobile struck after school bus driver motioned for pedestrian to cross street sued school district for negligence. The Circuit Court, 12th Judicial Circuit, Will County, Herman S. Haase, J., dismissed complaint. Pedestrian appealed. The Appellate Court, Breslin, J., held that defendants did not owe pedestrian duty.

Affirmed.

West Headnotes [Omitted....]

Opinion

Justice BRESLIN delivered the opinion of the court:

The plaintiffs, Janet L. Diaz and Jaime Diaz, filed this lawsuit against the defendants, Grace Krob (school bus driver) and Joliet Township High School District #204, for damages and loss of consortium from injuries Janet allegedly sustained when she was struck by an automobile after the school bus driver motioned for her to cross a street. The trial court dismissed the complaint finding that the defendants did not owe the plaintiffs a duty as a matter of law. We affirm.

The accident happened when Janet attempted to cross Collins Street, in Joliet, Illinois. The complaint alleged that as she proceeded west within the cross-walk, the "Don't Walk" warning sign activated. Thus, she stopped at the median dividing traffic on the street. At that point, the school bus driver, who was stopped immediately to the north of the crosswalk at the red light, motioned or waved to the plaintiff to continue walking across the street in front of the bus.

The complaint further alleged that the bus driver knew or should have known that the bus prevented the plaintiff from seeing traffic proceeding south on Collins Street in the lane nearest the curb. The complaint also alleged that as a proximate result of the bus driver's negligence in gesturing to the plaintiff to continue walking across the street the plaintiff suffered an injury when she was struck by a vehicle.

In response to these allegations, the defendants filed a motion to dismiss pursuant to section 2-615 of the Civil Practice Law (735 ILCS 5/2-615 (West 1992)) alleging that the plaintiffs failed to allege sufficient facts to give rise to a duty. The trial court agreed with the defendants and dismissed the complaint.

*99 [1] [2] A motion to dismiss under section 2-615 admits all well-pleaded facts in the complaint for purposes of the motion. (*Sisk v. Williamson County* (1994), 261 Ill.App.3d 49, 198 Ill.Dec. 342, 632 N.E.2d 672.) A cause of action will not be dismissed on the pleadings unless it clearly appears that no set of facts can be proved which will entitle **1233 ***801 the plaintiff to recover. (*Charles Hester Enterprises, Inc. v. Illinois Founders Insurance Co.* (1986), 114 Ill.2d 278, 102 Ill. Dec. 306, 499 N.E.2d 1319.)

[3] [4] [5] One of the necessary elements of a negligence cause of action is the existence of a duty which requires a person to conform to a certain standard of conduct for the purpose of protecting the plaintiff from an unreasonable risk of harm. (*Swett v. Village of Algonquin* (1988), 169 Ill. App. 3d 78, 119 Ill.Dec. 838, 523 N.E.2d 594; *Mitchell v. City of Chicago* (1991), 221 Ill. App.3d 1017, 164 Ill. Dec. 506, 583 N.E.2d 60.) It is not sufficient that the plaintiff's complaint merely alleges that a duty exists; the plaintiff must state facts from which the law will raise a duty. (*Swett*, 169 Ill.App.3d 78, 119 Ill.Dec. 838, 523 N.E.2d 594.) Factors relevant in determining whether a duty exists include: the foreseeability of injury, the likelihood of injury, the magnitude of the burden of guarding against the injury, the consequence of placing that burden on the defendant, and the possible seriousness of the injury. (*Deibert v. Bauer Brothers Construction Co.* (1990), 141 Ill.2d 430, 152 Ill.Dec. 552, 566 N.E. 2d 239.) Whether a duty exists is a question of law to be determined by the court. *Mitchell*, 221 Ill. App.3d 1017, 164 Ill.Dec. 506, 583 N.E.2d 60.

[6] The parties assert that the issue of whether a duty exists under the circumstances of this case is one of first impression in Illinois. The parties cite various out-of-state rulings in support of their respective positions. (See *Sweet v. Ringwelski* (1961), 362 Mich. 138, 106 N.W.2d 742; *Peka v.*

Boose (1988), 172 Mich.App. 139, 431 N.W.2d 399; *Valdez v. Bernard* (1986), 123 A.D.2d 351, 506 N.Y.S. 2d 363.)

In *Sweet,* the Michigan Supreme Court held that the trial court should not have granted a directed verdict in favor of the defendant truck driver on the ground of no showing of negligence. The defendant truck driver had stopped his truck and waved for the ten-year-old plaintiff pedestrian to cross the street on the crosswalk in front of him. The plaintiff continued crossing the street into the lane next to the truck and was struck by a car. The court's decision was based on the fact that the plaintiff was only ten years old, that her vision may have been obscured by the defendant's truck, and that she relied on what she considered to be directions from an adult.

In *Peka,* the defendant motioned for a southbound motorist to make a left turn. The southbound motorist followed the defendant's signal and struck the plaintiff's vehicle. The Michigan Appellate Court found that the signaling motorist owed no duty to the plaintiff. *100 The court found that *Sweet* was easily distinguishable on the basis that it involved a ten-year-old child who relied on the directions of an adult. The court found that the *Sweet* case should be limited to its facts.

In *Valdez,* the plaintiff was injured when she crossed a street after a bus driver had motioned for her to do so. The New York court noted that under certain circumstances, a driver of a motor vehicle may be liable to a pedestrian where that driver undertakes to direct a pedestrian safely across the road in front of his vehicle and negligently carries out that duty. The court found, however, that the bus driver was not the proximate cause of the plaintiff's injury where the plaintiff interpreted the bus driver's wave to mean only that he would not move the bus while the plaintiff passed in front of it.

Applying the above-mentioned principles and case law, we hold that the trial court correctly found as a matter of law that the defendants did not owe the plaintiffs a duty under the facts of this case. Unlike the cases cited by the parties, the crosswalk at the intersection in question was controlled by a "Don't Walk" signal. Nonetheless, the instant plaintiff chose to ignore it and proceed across the remainder of the intersection. Unlike *Sweet,* the plaintiff was not a youngster who relied on the directions of an adult. While we agree that *Sweet* is good law, we do not go as far as *Valdez* where it is implied that a duty would exist if the plaintiff interpreted the bus driver's gesture as something more than an indication that the driver would not move the bus until the plaintiff passed.

We agree that an injury is foreseeable here. But whether a legal duty exists involves **1234 ***802 more than just foreseeability of possible harm; it also involves legal and social policies. (*Swett,* 169 Ill.App.3d 78, 119 Ill.Dec. 838, 523 N.E.2d 594.) Here, the magnitude of guarding against the injury and the consequence of placing that burden on the defendant weigh heavily in favor of finding no duty. An adult pedestrian with no obvious impairments should be held responsible for deciding whether gestures and directions given by a motorist can be safely followed. We simply do not believe that the instant bus driver's act of common courtesy should be transformed into a tort thereby giving the plaintiff license to proceed across an intersection against a warning light and without taking any precautions of her own.

For the forgoing reasons, the judgment of the circuit court of Will County is affirmed.

Affirmed.

B. SECONDARY SOURCES OF LAW

Secondary sources are scholarly works or compilations of sources that help explain the law; they are not laws in themselves. Such authorities may include encyclopedias, annotations, treatises, restatements of the law, and American Law Reports (A.L.R.), among others.

C. INTERNATIONAL LAW

Many of today's lawyers will end up practicing law on a global level. The international system of law is too large a topic to cover here and you will probably not have occasion to apply international law in your first year of law school. However, it is worth remembering that the U.S. legal system is one of many. Should your career in law involve practicing internationally, you may become familiar with sources of law like those that come from treaties that govern legal relationships between countries, the United Nations Charter, or the International Court of Justice. While the legal systems of most American states are based on common law, many countries, including France and Spain, follow a civil law system where the central source of law comes from codes and statutes. Religious law is another kind of legal system that is followed in countries such as Saudi Arabia and Iran. Many legal systems have a hybrid or combination of common and civil law or civil and religious law.

PART II

CASE FILE 1
State v. Potter

CHAPTER 5

Introduction to Case File 1

This textbook will use three different case files to teach you legal analysis and writing. Each case file will require you to learn and practice skills that you will need as a lawyer. The case files will become increasingly more complex. The learning will be recursive. Case files 2 and 3 will require you to practice the skills you learned from case file 1 and perform the skills required of a more complex case file.

Case file 1 involves a client who has been arrested for driving under the influence (DUI) in New Hampshire. As you will see from the facts and the assigning memorandum, you are asked to address only one issue in a brief memorandum. You will only be drafting the issue and discussion of an objective office memorandum, not the entire memorandum. Case files 2 and 3 will require that you write entire objective office memoranda. In the process of writing the issue and discussion for case file 1, you will learn these skills:

- Reading and understanding a statute
- Close case reading
- Briefing a case
- Deconstructing and synthesizing case law to form a rule
- Identifying key client facts
- Structuring an office memorandum: parts of a memorandum
- Formulating and writing an issue
- Writing an outline of the discussion section
- Organizing an analysis, including explaining the rule and applying the rule
- Writing the legal discussion of an objective interoffice memorandum

MEMORANDUM

To: Law Intern
From: Supervising Attorney
Date: XXX
Re: *State v. Potter*—**Driving Under the Influence**

As you know, Dr. George Potter is our client and we have represented him in a number of matters. Recently, he was stopped and arrested for Driving Under the Influence in New Hampshire. There is no question that the breathalyzer is correct, that Potter is an adult, and that Potter was intoxicated when he was found asleep in his truck. The only issue that you should address is whether Potter was "driving." Potter was asleep in his car when he was stopped. The facts are included below.

From prior cases, I know that the cases I attached here are the key cases on this issue. Please use **only** the New Hampshire statute and the *O'Malley*, *Holloran*, and *Winstead* cases included here.

Facts

Dr. George Potter, a local doctor, wants to know whether he can be convicted of driving under the influence (DUI). Dr. Potter provided the following facts in an interview with our firm.

On Friday, August 6, 2013 Potter had a difficult day at the office because he was having administrative issues. Potter went to a local bar in Manchester near his office and had a few drinks. He left the bar at about 9 o'clock and started driving home to Concord, NH, twenty minutes away.

On his way home, Potter became very tired, and realized that he was on the verge of falling asleep. He pulled off the highway into a rest area, where he noticed several tractor trailer trucks and a few recreational vehicles parked.

Potter fell asleep in his truck. The truck had a raised cover over the back of the truck. Avid campers, Potter and his wife had outfitted the truck so that they had containers to store food, beverages, clothing, gear as well as a place to sleep. They had camped in their truck during their recent vacation. When he fell asleep, Potter's keys were in the ignition, his lights were on, and he was asleep in the driver's seat. The night was warm but not hot; Potter had the windows up to keep out insects.

An officer tapped on Potter's window, waking him up. She showed her identification, and asked him if he was okay. At some point, Potter remembers the officer telling him that she saw empty beer bottles in the back of Potter's truck, and that she smelled alcohol on his breath. She said that the hood of the truck was warm, and asked Potter to step out of it onto the pavement. Once Potter was out of his truck, the officer asked him to perform some field sobriety tests. Potter does not remember exactly what he was asked to do; however, he thinks he had to walk in a straight line for one of them. The officer then took Potter to the police station and gave him a breathalyzer test. Potter was told he had a blood alcohol content of 0.09 and was charged with driving under the influence.

NH DUI STATUTE

Revised Statutes Annotated of the State of New Hampshire Currentness

Title XXI. Motor Vehicles (Refs & Annos)

📖 Chapter 265-A. Alcohol or Drug Impairment (Refs & Annos)

📖 Driving or Operating Under the Influence of Drugs or Liquor

→ **265-A:2 Driving or Operating Under Influence of Drugs or Liquor; Driving or Operating With Excess Alcohol Concentration.**

I. No person shall drive or attempt to drive a vehicle upon any way or operate or attempt to operate an OHRV:

120 (a) While such person is under the influence of intoxicating liquor or any controlled drug or any combination of intoxicating liquor and controlled drugs; or

120 (b) While such person has an alcohol concentration of 0.08 or more or in the case of a person under the age of 21, 0.02 or more.

II. No person shall operate or attempt to operate a boat while under the influence of intoxicating liquor or a controlled drug or any combination of intoxicating liquor and a controlled drug or drugs, or while such person has an alcohol concentration of 0.08 or more or in the case of persons under the age of 21, 0.02 or more.

Updated with laws currently effective May 6, 2010 through Chapter 8 of the 2010 Reg. Sess., not including changes and corrections made by the State of New Hampshire, Office of Legislative Services.

Supreme Court of New Hampshire.

The STATE of New Hampshire
v.
John T. O'MALLEY.
No. 79-374.

June 25, 1980.

Defendant was convicted before the Trial Court, Rockingham County, Randall, J., of operating a motor vehicle while under the influence of intoxicating liquor and of operating a motor vehicle after a license had been revoked, and he appealed. The Supreme Court, King, J., held that absent evidence establishing beyond a reasonable doubt that defendant operated the subject motor vehicle, which was parked on public way with the engine running and with defendant asleep behind the wheel, defendant's mere presence in the nonmoving vehicle was insufficient to establish that he "operated" the vehicle.

Reversed.

Bois, J., filed dissenting opinion.

West Headnotes

[1] Automobiles 48A ⬤— 326

48A Automobiles
  48AVII Offenses
    48AVII(A) In Georgeral
      48Ak326 k. License and Registration.
Most Cited Cases

Automobiles 48A ⬤— 332

48A Automobiles
  48AVII Offenses
    48AVII(A) In Georgeral
      48Ak332 k. Driving While Intoxicated.
Most Cited Cases
For purpose of offenses of operating a motor vehicle while under the influence of intoxicating liquor and of operating a vehicle after a license has been revoked the court is reluctant to conclude that a defendant has "operated" a vehicle when, in fact, the police officer has not seen him behind the wheel moving the car forward. RSA 262:27-b, 262-A:62.

[2] Automobiles 48A ⬤— 355(2)

48A Automobiles
  48AVII Offenses
    48AVII(B) Prosecution
      48Ak355 Weight and Sufficiency of Evidence
        48Ak355(2) k. License and Registration.
Most Cited Cases

Automobiles 48A ⬤— 355(6)

48A Automobiles
  48AVII Offenses
    48AVII(B) Prosecution
      48Ak355 Weight and Sufficiency of Evidence
        48Ak355(6) k. Driving While Intoxicated.
Most Cited Cases
Circumstantial evidence which excludes any other rational conclusion is sufficient to establish beyond a reasonable doubt that a person was the "operator" of an automobile for purpose of offenses of operating a motor vehicle while under the influence of intoxicating liquor and of operating a motor vehicle after a license has been revoked. RSA 262:27-b, 262-A:62.

[3] Automobiles 48A ⬤— 355(2)

48A Automobiles
  48AVII Offenses
    48AVII(B) Prosecution
      48Ak355 Weight and Sufficiency of Evidence
        48Ak355(2) k. License and Registration.
Most Cited Cases

Automobiles 48A ⬤— 355(6)

48A Automobiles
  48AVII Offenses
    48AVII(B) Prosecution
      48Ak355 Weight and Sufficiency of Evidence
        48Ak355(6) k. Driving While Intoxicated.
Most Cited Cases
Since defendant's testimony that he had not operated nor intended to operate the motor vehicle, that he had hitchhiked to host's house and that the host had suggested that defendant warm up the car so that the host could drive him home and that defendant started the engine and fell asleep at the wheel was not unreasonable and as the State

offered no contrary evidence, there was insufficient evidence to establish beyond a reasonable doubt that defendant "operated" the automobile for purpose of offense of operating a motor vehicle under the influence of intoxicating liquor and offense of operating a motor vehicle after a license has been revoked. RSA 262:27-b, 262-A:62.

[4] Automobiles 48A ●━ 355(6)

48A Automobiles
  48AVII Offenses
    48AVII(B) Prosecution
      48Ak355 Weight and Sufficiency of Evidence
        48Ak355(6) k. Driving While Intoxicated.
Most Cited Cases
To secure a conviction of operating a motor vehicle while under the influence of intoxicating liquor the state must prove beyond a reasonable doubt that defendant operated a motor vehicle on a public way while under the influence, and absent evidence establishing beyond a reasonable doubt that defendant operated the vehicle, his mere presence in a nonmoving vehicle is insufficient to meet the state's burden. RSA 262-A:62.
**1388 *508 Gregory H. Carter, Acting Atty. Gen. (Deborah J. Cooper, Asst. Atty. Gen. orally), for the State.

James A. Connor, Manchester, by brief and orally, for defendant.

KING, Justice.

This is an appeal from a verdict by the Trial Court (Randall, J.) finding the defendant guilty of operating a motor vehicle while under the influence of intoxicating liquor, second offense, RSA 262-A:62, and of operating a motor vehicle after a license had been revoked. RSA 262:27-b.

On March 17, 1978, police officers observed a vehicle parked on a public way. The officers testified that the vehicle engine was idling, that the lights were on, and that exhaust was coming from the tail pipe. The officers further testified that they observed the defendant in the driver's seat with his head slumped over and his eyes closed. After the officers knocked on the vehicle's window without a response from the defendant, they opened the door and observed several empty and full beer bottles and detected an odor of alcohol.

After being awakened by one of the officers, the defendant allegedly pushed in the clutch and tried to shift the gear. The defendant was then asked to step out of the car and produce his license and registration. Defendant responded that he had no license. The officer then assisted the defendant to the police vehicle as the defendant stumbled, staggered, and nearly fell. The officer performed field sobriety tests on the defendant. During the course of the balancing tests, defendant swayed 5-6 inches front to rear and almost fell. In the performance of the finger-to-nose test, the defendant twice missed his nose with both hands. The defendant was then placed under arrest for operating a motor vehicle while intoxicated, second offense, and for operating after revocation.

(1)(2) The primary issue on this appeal is whether the trial *509 court erred in ruling that the defendant had, in fact, operated the vehicle. This court is reluctant to conclude that a defendant has operated a vehicle when, in fact, the officer has not seen the operator behind the wheel moving the car forward. State v. Scanlon, 110 N.H. 179, 263 A.2d 669 (1970); see 7 Am.Jur.2d, Automobiles and Highway Traffic s 256 (1963). In the instant case, the uncontroverted evidence is that the defendant was asleep and the car was not moving. Circumstantial evidence which excludes any other rational conclusion is sufficient, however, to establish beyond a reasonable doubt that a person was the operator of an automobile. State v. Costello, 110 N.H. 182, 263 A.2d 671 (1970); see State v. Martin, 116 N.H. 47, 351 A.2d 52 (1976).

(3) Defendant testified that he had not operated nor intended to operate the motor vehicle, that he had hitchhiked to Arthur Lambro's house, and that at some time later that evening, Lambro suggested that the defendant "(g)o warm up the car and I'll get my coat and drive you home." He testified he went out to the car and fell asleep. We find that the defendant's account of what transpired was not unreasonable and note that the State offered no evidence to dispute defendant's testimony.

(4) The State must prove beyond a reasonable doubt that the defendant operated the motor vehicle upon a public way in this State while under the influence of intoxicating liquor. State v. Costello supra (dissenting opinion); see State v. Scanlon supra. We hold, as a matter of law, that in the absence of evidence which establishes beyond a reasonable doubt that the defendant operated the motor vehicle, the defendant's mere presence in a nonmoving vehicle is insufficient to meet the State's burden.

Reversed.

BOIS, J., dissenting; the others concurred.
BOIS, Justice, dissenting:
The record before us reveals not only that the defendant was in physical control of an operable vehicle, but that he attempted to operate it upon being awakened. Admittedly **1389 no one witnessed the operation, but this court has long held that "'(d)irect evidence that the defendant was observed in the act of operating the motor vehicle is not an indispensable requisite to prove his operation.' *State v. Costello*, 110 N.H. 182, 183, 263 A. 2d 671, 672 (1970)*, and '(c)ircumstantial evidence may be utilized as proof of a crime, and eyewitnesses to the offense charged are not essential.' *510 *State v. Davis*, 108 N.H. 45, 50, 226 A.2d 873, 877 (1967)*; 15 D. Blashfield, Automobile Law and Practice s 491.25 n.18 (1969, 1974 Supp.); see 9 J. Wigmore, Evidence s 2497 (3d ed., 1940)" *State v. Allen*, 114 N.H. 682, 683, 327 A.2d 715, 716 (1974)*; see also *State v. Standish*, 116 N.H. 483, 363 A.2d 404 (1976)*; *State v. Martin*, 116 N.H. 47, 351 A.2d 52 (1976)*; *State v. Craigue*, 115 N.H. 239, 338 A.2d 548 (1975)*.

The majority opinion seems to be based on a belief that the defendant's account of what transpired was not unreasonable and that the State offered no evidence to dispute his testimony.

It is established law that in our examination of the record we are bound by the indisputable principle that conflicts in the testimony are for the trier of fact. *State v. Berry*, 117 N.H. 352, 355, 373 A.2d 355, 357 (1977)*; *State v. Bergeron*, 115 N.H. 70, 74, 333 A.2d 721, 724 (1975)*; *State v. Reed*, 106 N.H. 140, 141, 207 A.2d 443, 444 (1965)*. "(I)t is axiomatic that the Trial Court..., who had an opportunity to observe and hear the defendant..., (is) in a better position to judge his capacity and evaluate his testimony...than an appellate court." *State v. Reed, supra at 145, 207 A.2d at 446.* "Questions regarding the credibility of witnesses and the weight to be given testimony are for the (court) to resolve." *Duby v. Osgood*, 120 N.H. 356, 415 A.2d 326 (1980)*. "(T)he factfinder is not bound to believe even uncontroverted evidence." *93 Clearing House, Inc. v. Khoury*, 120 N.H. —, 415 A.2d 671 (1980)*. "(T)he trier of fact is not bound by an expert's testimony even when it is uncontradicted." *State v. Rullo*, 120 N.H. 149, 412 A.2d 1009, 1012 (1980)*. Our caselaw makes it abundantly clear that the trier of fact may believe or disbelieve, accept or reject, in whole or in part any witness' testimony. It is therefore a question of credibility and not one of reasonableness.

"In reviewing on appeal a trial court's determination, the question presented is whether there is evidence in the record from which a reasonable person could reach the conclusion which the trial court did." *State v. Inselburg*, 114 N.H. 824, 830, 330 A.2d 457, 461 (1974)*. Findings of fact are binding on this court and "(o)n review, we will not substitute our own conclusions of fact if the (court's) findings could reasonably be made on the evidence." *Bourgeois v. Town of Bedford*, 120 N.H. 145, 412 A.2d 1021, 1024 (1980)*; *Duby v. Osgood*, 120 N.H. —, 415 A.2d 32 (1980)*.

I therefore conclude that the conviction of the defendant was warranted by the evidence in this case.

N.H., 1980.
State v. O'Malley
120 N.H. 507, 416 A.2d 1387

Supreme Court of New Hampshire.

The STATE of New Hampshire
v.
Patrick W. HOLLORAN.
No. 94-558.

Dec. 27, 1995.

Defendant was convicted before the Derry District Court, Warhall, J., of driving while intoxicated, and he appealed. The Supreme Court held that evidence was sufficient to find that defendant was in actual physical control of his truck, as required by conviction, not withstanding that truck was legally parked, its lights were off, and engine was not running.

Affirmed.

West Headnotes

Automobiles 48A ☞ 355(6)

48A Automobiles
   48AVII Offenses
      48AVII(B) Prosecution
         48Ak355 Weight and Sufficiency of Evidence
         48Ak355(6) k. Driving While Intoxicated.
Most Cited Cases
Evidence in prosecution for driving while intoxicated was sufficient to find that defendant was in actual physical control of truck in which he was found, not withstanding that truck was legally parked, its lights were off, and engine was not running; when officer came upon truck, defendant was in the driver's seat, keys were in the ignition, defendant exhibited signs of drunkenness, and told officer that he was waiting for a call to pick up his wife, who was in another town; rational trier of fact could find beyond a reasonable doubt that defendant would be imminently operating truck. RSA 259:24, 265:82.

**800 *563 Jeffrey R. Howard, Attorney Georgeral (Patrick E. Donovan, Assistant Attorney Georgeral, on the brief and orally), for State.

*564 Casassa & Ryan, Hampton (Kenneth D. Murphy, on the brief and orally), for defendant.

**801 MEMORANDUM OPINION

PER CURIAM.

After a bench trial, the Derry District Court (*Warhall,* J.) convicted the defendant, Patrick W. **Holloran**, of driving while intoxicated. *See* RSA 265:82, I (Supp.1994). On appeal, the defendant asserts that the trial court erred in denying his motion for a directed verdict based upon insufficiency of the evidence. We affirm.

In the evening of March 15, 1994, Londonderry Police Officer Mark Cagnetta approached a Chevrolet pickup truck with its lights off parked on Symmes Drive in Londonderry. The officer saw the defendant sitting alone behind the wheel. Cagnetta "spotlighted" the truck and the defendant quickly jumped out. Cagnetta told the defendant to get back into the truck, observing that the defendant appeared "unsteady" on his feet.

The defendant explained that he was waiting for a call from his wife to pick her up from a Tupperware party in Auburn. The officer did not see a phone, and the defendant indicated that he had a pager. Cagnetta noticed that the defendant's breath smelled of an alcoholic beverage, that his eyes were glassy and bloodshot, and that he appeared disheveled. The officer also observed that although the engine was not running, the keys to the truck were in the ignition. The defendant stated that he had been at the airport and had come to Symmes Drive to wait for his wife, but that he had had nothing to drink that evening and should have remained at the airport. After the defendant failed three field sobriety tests, Cagnetta arrested him for driving while under the influence of alcohol.

At the close of the State's case, the defendant moved for a directed verdict, arguing that the evidence was insufficient for a rational trier of fact to find, beyond a reasonable doubt, that he had driven his truck on the night of the arrest. The court denied the motion and found the defendant guilty, sentencing him to a fine, ninety-day license revocation, and mandatory attendance in an alcohol awareness program. This appeal followed.

The defendant was convicted of violating RSA 265:82. "The *actus reus* contemplated in RSA 265:82 is 'driv[ing]' a motor vehicle while under the influence of alcohol." *State v. Willard*, 139 N.H. 568, 570, 660 A.2d 1086, 1087 (1995). "Driv[ing]" has been defined as "operat[ing]" or being in "actual physical control" of a motor vehicle. RSA 259:24 (1993). Because the State does not allege that the defendant was operating his truck, the question before us is whether *565 a rational trier of fact, viewing the evidence most favorably to the State, could have found beyond a reasonable doubt that the defendant was in actual physical control of the truck.

"To have 'actual physical control' of a motor vehicle, one must have the capacity bodily to guide or exercise dominion over the vehicle at the present time." *Willard*, 139 N.H. at 571, 660 A.2d at 1088 (emphasis omitted). What constitutes "actual physical control" will vary depending upon the facts of the case, but "the primary focus of the inquiry is whether the person is merely using the vehicle as a stationary shelter or whether it is reasonable to assume that the person will, while under the influence, jeopardize the public by exercising some measure of control over the vehicle." *Atkinson v. State*, 331 Md. 199, 627 A.2d 1019, 1028 (1993.

At trial, the State adduced only circumstantial evidence to prove that the defendant had "actual physical control" of his truck. "[C]ircumstantial evidence which excludes any other rational conclusion is sufficient to establish beyond a reasonable doubt the *actus reus* set out in a motor vehicle statute." *Willard*, 139 N.H. at 571, 660 A.2d at 1088 (quotation and ellipses omitted). In applying this standard, "we examine each evidentiary item in the context of all the evidence, not in isolation." *State v. Bissonnette*, 138 N.H. 82, 85, 635 A.2d 468, 469 (1993).

The defendant argues that because the truck was legally parked, the lights were off, and the engine was not running, it is speculative to conclude that he would soon be operating the vehicle. These facts alone, however, are not dispositive. When Officer Cagnetta came upon the truck, the defendant was in the driver's seat. The defendant **802 exhibited signs of drunkenness, and he told the officer that he was waiting for a call to pick up his wife, who was in another town. The keys were in the ignition. In the context of the officer's observations and the defendant's statements, a rational trier of fact could find beyond a reasonable doubt that the defendant would be imminently operating the truck in an inebriated condition, and, therefore, that he was in actual physical control of the vehicle. See *Willard*, 139 N.H. at 571, 660 A.2d at 1088.

Affirmed.

BRODERICK. J., did not sit; the others concurred.
N.H.,1995.
State v. Holloran
140 N.H. 563, 669 A.2d 800

Supreme Court of New Hampshire.

The STATE of New Hampshire
v.
William T. WINSTEAD.
No. 2002-660.

Argued Oct. 9, 2003.
Opinion Issued Nov. 12, 2003.

Following a bench trial, defendant was convicted in the District Court, Claremont County, Yazinski, J., of driving while intoxicated (DWI). Defendant appealed. The Supreme Court, Duggan, J., held that sufficient evidence existed that defendant was in actual physical control of car before he fell asleep to support conviction.

Affirmed.

West Headnotes

[1] Criminal Law 110 ⊶1036.1(3.1)

110 Criminal Law
  110XXIV Review
    110XXIV(E) Presentation and Reservation in Lower Court of Grounds of Review
      110XXIV(E) 1 In Georgeral
        110 k1036 Evidence
          110 k1036.1 In Georgeral
            110 k1036.1(3) Particular Evidence
              110 k1036.1(3.1) k. In Georgeral.
Most Cited Cases

Criminal Law 110 ⊶ 1043(2)

110 Criminal Law
  110XXIV Review
    110XXIV(E) Presentation and Reservation in Lower Court of Grounds of Review
      110XXIV(E) 1 In Georgeral
        110k1043 Scope and Effect of Objection
          110k1043 (2) k. Necessity of Specific Objection. Most Cited Cases

Defendant failed to preserve for appellate review his claim that trial court erred by admitting blood test results in prosecution for driving while intoxicated (DWI), where defendant failed to make contemporaneous and specific objection to admission of blood test results. Rules of Evid., Rule 103(b)(1),

[2] Criminal Law 110 ⊶ 1030(2)

110 Criminal Law
  110XXIV Review
    110XXIV (E) Presentation and Reservation in Lower Court of Grounds of Review
      110XXIV (E) 1 In Georgeral
        110k1030 Necessity of Objections in Georgeral
          110k1030(2) k. Constitutional Questions. Most Cited Cases

Defendant failed to preserve for appellate review his claim that police officer violated defendant's right to equal protection by treating defendant differently in disturbing defendant in car when officer would typically not disturb people parked in recreation vehicle (RV) in parking lot, in prosecution for driving while intoxicated (DWI), although defense counsel made three references to different treatment afforded defendant's car than RV, where no constitutional argument was raised in trial court. U.S.C.A. Const.Amend. 14.

[3] Criminal Law 110 ⊶1030(2)

110 Criminal Law
  110XXIV Review
    110XXIV(E) Presentation and Reservation in Lower Court of Grounds of Review
      110XXIV(E) 1 In Georgeral
        110 k1030 Necessity of Objections in Georgeral
          110 k1030(2) k. Constitutional Questions. Most Cited Cases

Where defendant raises constitutional claim, it must be brought to attention of trial court in order to preserve issue for appeal.

[4] Automobiles 48A ⊶ 355(6)

48A Automobiles
  48AVII Offenses
    48AVII(B) Prosecution
      48Ak355 Weight and Sufficiency of Evidence
        48Ak355(6) k. Driving While Intoxicated.
Most Cited Cases

Sufficient circumstantial evidence existed that defendant was in actual physical control of car before he fell asleep to support conviction for driving while intoxicated (DWI); evidence indicated that officer found defendant asleep in vehicle with motor running in parking lot, and that defendant unlocked door, sat in driver's seat, pushed clutch in, moved gear selector to neutral, started engine, and turned on heater. RSA 259:24, 265:82.

[5] Automobiles 48A ☞ 332

48A Automobiles
  48AVII Offenses
    48AVII(A) In Georgeral
      48Ak332 k. Driving While Intoxicated.
Most Cited Cases
To have "actual physical control" of motor vehicle, for purposes of driving while intoxicated (DWI), one must have capacity bodily to guide or exercise dominion over vehicle at present time. RSA 259:23, 265:82 .
**776*245 Peter W. Heed, attorney General (Jonathan V. Gallo, assistant attorney General, on the brief and orally), for the State.

Nancy S. Tierney, of Lebanon, by brief and orally, for the defendant.

DUGGAN, J.

Following a bench trial in Claremont District Court (*Yazinski*, J.), the defendant, William T. Winstead, was found guilty of driving while intoxicated. *See* RSA 265:82 (Supp.2002). On appeal, he contends that: (1) the trial court erred when it admitted the results of his blood alcohol test; (2) he was denied equal protection of the law; and (3) the evidence was insufficient to prove he was in control of the vehicle. We affirm.

The record supports the following facts. The charge arose out of an incident on April 6, 2002, when, at approximately 3:13 a.m., Officer Shawn L. Hallock of the Claremont Police Department discovered the defendant in a car in the Wal-Mart parking lot. The defendant was sleeping upright in the driver's seat, with the car engine running. At trial, the defendant testified that he decided to sleep in his car because he was "not…capable to drive anywhere," and that the car was running

so he could stay warm. The defendant further testified that while he had no intention of driving the car, he did unlock the door, sit in the driver's seat, push the clutch in, move the gear selector to neutral, start the engine and turn on the heater.

Hallock approached the car and attempted to wake the defendant. When the defendant awoke and spoke with Hallock, Hallock "immediately smelled an odor of intoxicant." The defendant admitted to Hallock that he had consumed a six-pack of Bacardi Silvers that evening. Hallock asked the defendant to perform field sobriety tests, which the defendant failed. Hallock subsequently arrested the defendant for driving while intoxicated.

After his arrest, the defendant was taken to the Claremont Police Department where he read and signed the Administrative License Suspension form, which authorized the police to perform any combination of breath, blood, urine or physical testing. The defendant was first given an intoxilyzer breath test, which resulted in a blood alcohol content (BAC) of 0.07. The result of the defendant's intoxilyzer test was below the statutorily defined level (BAC of 0.08) for *prima facie* evidence of intoxication. *See* RSA 265:82. Hallock then asked the defendant to take a blood test. The defendant testified that Hallock requested a blood test only for drugs. The defendant's blood was tested for both drugs and alcohol, *246 which resulted in a BAC of 0.08. The results of both tests were admitted at trial without objection. The district court found the defendant guilty and denied his motion to reconsider. This appeal followed.

[1] On appeal, the defendant first argues that the district court erred in admitting the blood test results. The defendant contends that the police were not entitled to conduct further testing after the intoxilyzer test revealed a BAC of 0.07 and that the defendant consented only to a blood test for drugs, not alcohol. We conclude, however, that the issue was not preserved for appellate review.

"The General rule in this jurisdiction is that a contemporaneous and specific objection **777 is required to preserve an issue for appellate review." *State v. Brinkman,* 136 N.H. 716, 718, 621 A.2d 932 (1993) (quotation omitted). In addition, "[t]he objection must state 'explicitly the specific ground of objection.'" *Id.* (quoting *N.H. R. Ev.* 103(b)(1)). "This requirement, grounded in common sense and judicial economy, affords the trial court an opportunity to correct an error it may have made...." *Brinkman,* 136 N.H. at 718, 621 A.2d 932.

At trial, the State questioned Officer Hallock about the blood test performed on the defendant. The State then offered the certified lab results of the blood test as Exhibit 4. The following colloquy ensued:

[STATE]: State would enter Exhibit 4.

[COURT]: Any objection, Ms. Tierney?

[DEFENSE]: No, Your Honor.

Because the defendant failed to make "a contemporaneous and specific objection" to the admission of the blood test results, *id.,* the issue was not preserved for appellate review.

[2] The defendant next argues that his right to equal protection was violated because Officer Hallock testified that he does not typically disturb people parked in recreational vehicles (RVs) in the Wal-Mart parking lot. Thus, the defendant argues, he was treated differently because he was in a car. We conclude, however, that this issue was also not preserved for appellate review.

[3] "This court has consistently held that we will not consider issues raised on appeal that were not presented in the lower court." *State v. McAdams,* 134 N.H. 445, 447, 594 A.2d 1273 (1991) (quotation omitted). Where the defendant raises a constitutional claim, it must be brought to the attention of the trial court in order to preserve the issue for appeal. *State v. Patterson,* 145 N.H. 462, 466-67, 764 A.2d 901 (2000) .

*247 At trial, defense counsel made three references to the different treatment afforded the defendant's car as opposed to an RV. First, defense counsel questioned Officer Hallock on cross-examination about another RV present in the Wal-Mart parking lot on the night the defendant was arrested. Second, defense counsel questioned lOfficer Hallock about whether, in General, he would knock on the door of an RV that was running. Finally, as part of closing argument, the defense argued: "Officer Hallock indicated that if he had been in the RV, he would have never bothered. The mere fact he was in a Subaru, or a Saturn, is what caused his eyes to light up. The kind of vehicle you're in shouldn't be determinative." In addition, in a motion to reconsider, the defense stated that one "area[ ] of law to be reviewed" included "[w]ere there grounds for waking him if, according to testimony, he would not have been disturbed if he had been in an RV."

Aside from these General references to the different treatment afforded persons in cars and RVs, no constitutional argument was raised at the trial court. At no point during the trial or in the motion to reconsider did defense counsel assert that the defendant's right to equal protection was being violated. Because the defendant failed to "bring the constitutional claim to the attention of the trial court, the issue is not preserved for appeal, and we decline to review it." *Id.* at 467, 764 A.2d 901.

[4] Finally, the defendant argues that because he was asleep, only turned on the heat and had no intent to drive the car, there was insufficient evidence for the trial court to find that he was in control of the car and thus operating a vehicle under the influence. We must determine "whether a rational trier of fact ... could have found beyond a reasonable doubt that the defendant was in actual physical control of the ****778** [vehicle]." *State v. Holloran,* 140 N.H. 563, 564-65, 669 A.2d 800 (1995) (per curiam); *see* RSA 265:82; RSA 259:24 (1993).

[5] "To have 'actual physical control' of a motor vehicle, one must have the capacity bodily to guide or exercise dominion over the vehicle at the present time." *State v. Willard,* 139 N.H. 568, 571, 660 A.2d 1086 (1995) (emphasis omitted). While a person who is sound asleep cannot have such a capacity, "circumstantial evidence which excludes any other rational conclusion is sufficient...to establish beyond a reasonable doubt

the *actus reus* set out in a motor vehicle statute." *Id.* (quotation omitted).

This case is indistinguishable from *Willard*. In *Willard*, the defendant was found asleep in the driver's seat of his vehicle in a parking lot with the vehicle's engine idling. A police officer woke him, determined he was intoxicated and arrested him for driving while intoxicated. In holding that *248 a rational trier of fact could find that the defendant was in *actual physical control* of the vehicle, we noted that "if circumstantial evidence were to prove that [the] defendant [ ] started his car before falling asleep, he would have been in actual physical control of it while awake and in the driver's seat." *Id.;* see also <u>Atknson v. State, 331 Md. 199, 627 A.2d 1019, 1028 (1993)</u> ("Indeed, once an individual has started the vehicle, he or she has come as close as possible to actually [operating it] without doing so and will generally be in 'actual physical control' of the vehicle.").

Here, the defendant was also found asleep in the driver's seat of a car in a parking lot with the engine running. Moreover, the defendant testified at trial that he unlocked the door, sat in the driver's seat, pushed the clutch in, moved the gear selector to neutral, started the engine and turned on the heater. Given these facts and the reasonable inferences therefrom, a rational trier of fact could find beyond a reasonable doubt that the defendant was in actual physical control of the car before he fell asleep. *See* <u>*Willard* 139 N.H. at 571, 660 A.2d 1086</u>.

Affirmed.

<u>BROCK</u>, C.J., and <u>BRODERICK</u>, <u>NADEAU</u> and <u>DALIANIS</u>, JJ., concurred.
N.H.,2003.
State v. Winstead
      150H. 244, 836 A.2d

A. ADDRESSING THE CLIENT'S PROBLEM

As we know, a legal analysis begins with a client's problem. Most clients, whether they are individuals, businesses, organizations, or government entities, will come to you with a story, a set of facts, and ask you for your expert advice or information about how to proceed. The steps you take to help your client may vary depending on the particular situation. Remember, solving your client's problem is a recursive process, not a linear process. Generally, here are the steps you will go through:

1. Understand the facts of your client's case.
2. Identify the area of law that is likely to hold the answer (e.g., employment law, medical malpractice law, criminal law)
3. Research law. This might start with reading a treatise or other secondary source.
4. Read and study relevant statutes and cases.
5. Identify the key fact from case law or legal principles that apply to your client's problem.
6. Review client's facts and identify the key decisive facts.
7. Narrow the body of legal authority that addresses your client's problem—winnow out authority that is not on point.
8. Outline legal analysis.
9. Begin writing process. Once you are ready to write, you will embark on another multistep process required to complete a legal analysis. These steps are introduced on page 83.

In Dr. Potter's case, the exact legal issue has been given to you. In real practice, you would have had to figure out that the issue is whether he was "driving" under the statute. Here your supervisor has already done that part. She has also given you the cases and the statute. So, steps 1 through 3 have been done. What follows will help you with the remaining steps.

B. CASE FILE 1: READING AND UNDERSTANDING A STATUTE

In the Potter facts, you learned that the client was charged in New Hampshire with driving under the influence. You will learn how to find a statute in your legal research class. Once you have found it, you will have to study it and identify what the statute actually prohibits.

Recall that statutes come from the legislative branch of government. What is contained in a statute is law. Statutory law (from the legislature) or regulatory law (from agencies) can govern criminal conduct and civil conduct. Although case file 1 does not require you to examine a regulation, it is helpful to remember that in any given legal problem, your research may lead you to a statute, which in turn leads you to a regulation. Regulatory rules are enacted by agencies to carry out laws enacted by the legislature (either state or federal). Remember the woman who believes she was fired because of her age? The employer's conduct would be regulated by federal or state statutes or regulations that govern civil behavior.

 The legislature or the agencies do not necessarily have the last word on what the law is as it is applied to individuals or businesses. The United States operates under a common law system and, thus, it is up to the courts to interpret statutes and regulations once litigants raise questions about them. Litigants can challenge statutes for a variety of reasons, including that they are unconstitutional. Or, litigants can take issue with words or phrases in a statute that are arguably ambiguous. This type of claim usually occurs when a litigant believes that the statute as applied to his or her situation has been applied incorrectly or illegally.

Thus, challenges to statutes do not arise in a vacuum; they arise because the statute has been applied to litigants in a way that they believe is unlawful. A particular law may apply to a multitude of factual situations. Let's take the New Hampshire DUI statute. In our case, the police observed Dr. Potter in a car that was not moving. Can the statute apply if it prohibits "driving" under the influence? To answer this, you have to study how the legislature defines "driving." Then, you have to study how the courts have applied the legislature's definition of "driving."

The statute also prohibits driving "on any way" while under the influence. Although this is not the issue we have been asked to examine, what if Dr. Potter was on a private dirt road? Or, what if he had pulled off the highway so he was on the grassy area next to the highway? Would his conduct be illegal under the statute? To answer this, you would have to study what the legislature meant by "any way." First, you would look up the definition of a "way" in the definitional section of the statutory code. If there was no definition, or if the definition still did not clarify the question, then, as above, you would have to study the case law to see how the courts have applied the legislature's definition in other circumstances.

Let's take a close look at the statute that will decide Dr. Potter's fate:

This is name the legislature has given the state statutes

NH DUI STATUTE

Revised Statutes Annotated of the State of New Hampshire <u>Currentness</u>

The statutes are divided into "Titles" and "Chapters"

Title XXI. Motor Vehicles (<u>Refs & Annos</u>)

🗐 <u>Chapter 265-A.</u> Alcohol or Drug Impairment (<u>Refs & Annos</u>)

This is the specific name of the DUI statute

🗐 Driving or Operating Under the Influence of Drugs or Liquor

→ **265-A:2 Driving or Operating Under Influence of Drugs or Liquor; Driving or Operating With Excess Alcohol Concentration.**

I. No person shall drive or attempt to drive a vehicle upon any way or operate or attempt to operate an OHRV:

(a) While such person is under the influence of intoxicating liquor or any controlled drug or any combination of intoxicating liquor and controlled drugs; or

(b) While such person has an alcohol concentration of 0.08 or more or in the case of a person under the age of 21, 0.02 or more.

Note that the statute prohibits two types of conduct: "driving a vehicle" and "operating a boat"

II. No person shall operate or attempt to operate a boat while under the influence of intoxicating liquor or a controlled drug or any combination of intoxicating liquor and a controlled drug or drugs, or while such person has an alcohol concentration of 0.08 or more or in the case of persons under the age of 21, 0.02 or more.

Updated with laws currently effective May 6, 2010 through Chapter 8 of the 2010 Reg. Sess., not including changes and corrections made by the State of New Hampshire, Office of Legislative Services.

Under this statute, a person can commit DUI of a vehicle or a boat in two different ways. Under section (a), a person can be guilty of DUI if he or she is under the influence of alcohol or controlled drugs. Under section (b), a person violates the statute if the concentration of alcohol is over .08, or, in the case of someone under 21, more than .02.

Most statutes can be deconstructed into specific elements. One way to think about elements is to ask: "What must the government (or state) prove?" or "What must a 'plaintiff' prove?" Here, the statute requires that all four of the elements must be met, although there are alternative ways to meet the statute (e.g., boat or vehicle). This formulation—requiring a number of elements be met—is called **conjunctive**. Where there are alternative ways to meet a statute, the formulation is called **disjunctive**. The New Hampshire DUI statute is a good example of a law that incorporates both. To violate the statute, an individual must "drive or attempt to drive a vehicle upon any way or operate or attempt to operate an OHRV" AND either fit within subsection (a) OR subsection (b).

The "AND" represents a conjunctive portion of the statute and the "OR" represents a disjunctive portion. When you are breaking down a statute and identifying what it requires, look for whether the elements are disjunctive or conjunctive.

PRACTICAL TIP

Many states have model jury instructions. These are templates that judges use when instructing a jury about what they must find in a particular case. Jury instructions are usually written by a committee of state bar members and judges. The instructions typically outline the elements of a crime (in a criminal case) or cause of action (in a civil case). They are usually available on line or through the state's Bar association. This is a good resource to use in identifying elements.

Notice how each of these elements contains terms that may need further defining: "operating," "way," and perhaps "vehicle" or "boat." State statutes include a definitional section. Usually this appears at the beginning of a particular title or chapter, or it can appear at the beginning of the entire statutory code. For example, in New Hampshire, the words "operate" and "way" are defined in the beginning of the title. Part of understanding a statute includes checking if particular words or phrases have been defined by the legislature in the appropriate definitional section.

C. HOW DO COURTS INTERPRET STATUTES?

A significant amount of a lawyer's time is spent analyzing a court's interpretation of a statute. Courts follow some basic rules when they interpret and apply statutes. These are known as the Canons of Construction. Here is a brief description of the most widely used rules:

- *Plain Meaning Rule.* The court will look at the actual words of the statute and apply a common, ordinary meaning. Sometimes a court will use a dictionary definition of a common word to identify its meaning.
- *Legislative Intent.* The court will examine documents (e.g., hearing minutes, committee reports, or preambles) to discern what the legislators' goals were in drafting the statute. Sometimes a court will examine other parts of a statute, or the statute as a whole, to discover the legislative intent.
- *Stare Decisis.* The court may examine lower courts' interpretations of the statute or interpretations of similar statutes from other states.

After you have a good understanding of the statute, the next step is to examine whether the statute applies to your facts. Is the statute a good fit given your client's facts? What questions do you have about how it might apply? This inquiry will likely point you toward case law and thus the next step is to read cases where the court has applied the statute's terms. In the case of Dr. Potter, we are interested in the term "drive."

CASE FILE 1: Assignment—Understanding a Statute

1. Study the New Hampshire DUI statute. Outline the elements that are required for conviction under the statute.
2. If Dr. Potter was not a doctor, but was a 16-year-old high school student, which elements would be relevant? What would the state have to prove in this instance?

D. CASE FILE 1: BRIEFING CASES AND CLOSE CASE READING

1. Briefing a Case

Careful case reading and effective case briefing are skills you will use throughout your career. At first, your case briefs will follow a format suggested to you. As you progress through law school and in your legal employment, you will likely adapt your briefing format to a style that works for you. You may find that the way you brief a case for your classes is different than how you brief cases you read for a research project. What follows is a suggested format. At first, briefing a case will take you a long time. As you get used to it, the process will go faster, but don't try to rush through. Careful, almost forensic, reading and analysis is at the very core of good lawyering.

a. Why Brief Cases?

- Because briefing forces you to study the case and condense its most important information.
- Because briefing helps you organize the cases. This is especially true when your research project involves numerous cases.
- Because briefing helps you to efficiently refer to cases as you are writing your memorandum.

b. General Tips on Briefing

- It will be time consuming at first. Have patience because soon you will be briefing cases more quickly.
- Study cases you read for a research project in the same way you study a case to prepare for a class. Re-read the case several times, highlighting and taking notes about what you are reading.
- Remember that the headnotes at the beginning of an opinion are not part of the opinion and are not written by the court.
- Resist the impulse to use a lot of quotes. Try to put the case information in your own words. This will help ensure that you understand what the court is saying.

c. Parts of a Case Brief

1. Name, date, court
2. Procedural history
3. Facts
4. Issue(s)
5. Holding
6. Reasoning
7. Disposition
8. Comments/dicta

d. Parts of a Case Brief in Detail

i. Name of the Case, Date, Court

- Use *Bluebook* form where possible. Be sure to note the date of the decision. Identify what level of court the case comes out of. Cross reference in the *Bluebook* index to understand the hierarchy of courts if the case is from a state court.
- Understand the players.
  - Plaintiff = person who brought the lawsuit
  - Defendant = person being sued or charged criminally
  - Appellant = person who lost in lower court and brings appeal
  - Appellee = person who won below and responds to appeal
  - Petitioner = person petitioning court to hear appeal
  - Respondent = person responding to the appeal

ii. Procedural History

- Identify what occurred in the lower court to cause this case to be in the present court. Usually you can find this information at the beginning of the case.

iii. Facts
- Include facts that give the case context.
- Include the decisive facts upon which the court's holding rests. These are often found at the end of the opinion where the court gives its holding.

iv. Issue
- Identify the legal question the court is resolving. You can frame this as a question for which there is a yes or no answer.

v. Holding
- The court's decision on the question that was actually before it.
- The holding directly answers the question presented in the issue.
- Characterize the parties to state the decision in its broadest terms. (Example: Instead of "Mr. Jones can sue..." you would state the holding as "A father can sue...")

vi. Reasoning
- Identify the reasons given by the court for reaching its decision, including explicit and implicit reasoning.
- Identify what types of reasoning the court uses.
- The reasoning explains why the court ruled the way it did.
- Often the reasoning combines decisive facts and the legal issue.

vii. Disposition
- Identify what the court specifically did.
  - Did it reverse the lower court's ruling? Remand the case? Affirm the lower court's decision?
  - Understand the key terms: reverse, remand, reconsideration, affirm.

viii. The Rule
- Identify the rule from the case.
  - Combine the holding and the reasoning to ascertain the rule.
  - What is the general legal principle, applicable to the particular factual circumstance that the case stands for?
  - The rule may not be clearly stated, in which case you need to infer the rule by putting together the decisive facts, the holding, and the reasoning.

ix. Comments/Dicta
- "Comments" are comments you might write to yourself about something you do not understand in the case, or something that seems interesting or thought provoking that you want to ask about.

- "Dicta" is extra language in the opinion that is not part of the holding. It may touch upon a legal issue, but if it does not directly address the issue before the court; it is dicta and not law.
- Dicta might be in the form of a policy statement the court wants to make.
- Dicta can sometimes be a good indication of what the court may do in future cases.

CASE FILE 1: Assignment—Case Briefing and Close Case Reading

Using the format described above, write case briefs of *State v. Winstead*, *State v. Holloran*, and *State v. O'Malley* (in case file 1).

2. Studying a Case

When judges decide cases and write opinions, they do not operate in a world untethered from particular facts, precedent, or social policy. They may conform to past decisions, or they may decide to change old law. Every case is decided because a specific set of facts is before the court. And, every case is decided within the social construct and norms existing at the time an opinion is written. Opinions are not always explicitly clear, and you may have to figure out what a court is saying by studying the opinion carefully and reading between the lines for implicit reasoning.

Sometimes the reasoning the court uses seems convoluted. This may be more likely to happen in a case where the court wanted to reach a certain result and had to bend the reasoning to get there. Sometimes courts decide cases and give very little justification for the ruling. If you are confused by a court's opinion, don't automatically assume that you are missing something. It might be that the reasoning or the holding is hard to discern. Law students are often surprised at how long it can take to read and comprehend even a short case.

> **PRACTICAL TIP**
>
> Most of the time you will read cases on screens. BE VERY CAREFUL that you read the *entire court's opinion* (the headnotes are not part of the opinion), all the way to the end. Do not skim or jump from page to page. Not reading the entire case, page by page, runs a potentially dangerous risk of missing a key point.

When you read cases online be careful that you don't miss parts. Be sure to read *everything* the court says. For example, a court may begin a case by running through the facts. However, the holding—and remember that the holding will likely appear toward the end of the case—may only rely on one or two of these facts. To understand the holding, you will need to be sure that you understand the **decisive facts**, not just the overall facts of the case. The court may acknowledge an important policy or societal concern at the end of an opinion or in the middle. Think of yourself as an investigator in the sense that you need to comb through and identify all the key points in a case that help you solve your client's problem.

3. Breaking Down a Case

a. Identifying Parts of a Case: Citation, Caption, Date, Summary, and Headnotes

Let's take a look at the *O'Malley* case. To start, look at the caption and the summary:

This is the case citation. State appellate cases are published in two reporters, an official state reporter, and an official regional reporter. The first number is the reporter volume and the second number is the page number.

These are the names of the parties. The state is a party because this is a criminal case brought against an individual.

This is the date the case was decided.

The first paragraph is a summary of the case that includes what happened procedurally. The summary is written by editors, not by the court.

This is the ultimate holding— what the court did. "Bois" is the name of the judge who dissented.

These are "Headnotes" written by the publisher, West. Their purpose is to help with research. They are not written by the court and do not constitute the court's opinion. Neither the summary paragraph above nor the headnotes should ever be cited to or relied on as legal authority.

120 N.H. 507, 416 A.2D 1387

Supreme Court of New Hampshire.

The STATE of New Hampshire
v.
John T. O'MALLEY.
No. 79-374.

June 25, 1980.

Defendant was convicted before the Trial Court, Rockingham County, Randall, J., of operating a motor vehicle while under the influence of intoxicating liquor and of operating a motor vehicle after a license had been revoked, and he appealed. The Supreme Court, King, J., held that absent evidence establishing beyond a reasonable doubt that defendant operated the subject motor vehicle, which was parked on public way with the engine running and with defendant asleep behind the wheel, defendant's mere presence in the nonmoving vehicle was insufficient to establish that he "operated" the vehicle.

Reversed.

Bois, J., filed dissenting opinion.

West Headnotes

[1] **Automobiles 48A** ⚬— 326

48A Automobiles
    48AVII Offenses
        48AVII(A) In Georgeral
            48Ak326 k. License and Registration. Most Cited Cases

Automobiles 48A ◆— 332

<u>48A</u> Automobiles

   <u>48AVII</u> Offenses

      <u>48AVII(A)</u> In Georgeral

         <u>48Ak332</u> k. Driving While Intoxicated. <u>Most Cited Cases</u>

For purpose of offenses of operating a motor vehicle while under the influence of intoxicating liquor and of operating a vehicle after a license has been revoked the court is reluctant to conclude that a defendant has "operated" a vehicle when, in fact, the police officer has not seen him behind the wheel moving the car forward. RSA 262:27-b, 262-A:62.

This is "star pagination." The double star tells you that this is the page number in the regional reporter. The single star refers to the page in the state reporter. Use in your case briefs for ease of reference.

* * *

**1388 *508 Gregory H. Carter, Acting Atty. Gen. (Deborah J. Cooper, Asst. Atty. Gen. orally), for the State.

James A. Connor, Manchester, by brief and orally, for defendant.

These are the names of the lawyers who wrote the briefs.

KING, Justice.

This is the Justice who wrote the court's opinion.

This is an appeal from a verdict by the Trial Court (Randall, J.) finding the defendant guilty of operating a motor vehicle while under the influence of intoxicating liquor, second offense, RSA 262-A:62, and of operating a motor vehicle after a license had been revoked. RSA 262:27-b.

This, along with any dissent or concurrence, is the opinion. This is the only text you can rely on and cite to in your analysis.

b. The Procedural History

The procedural history of the case is usually in the beginning of the court's opinion. It explains what happened in the case before it came before the appellate court for review. Typically, the procedural review will include the particular issues the parties have raised for the appellate court's review. In the *Winstead* case, the procedural history is in the beginning of the case:

> Following a bench trial in Claremont District Court (*Yazinski*, J.), the defendant, William T. Winstead, was found guilty of driving while intoxicated. *See* <u>RSA 265:82</u> (Supp.2002). On appeal, he contends that: (1) the trial court erred when it admitted the results of his blood alcohol test; (2) he was denied equal protection of the law; and (3) the evidence was insufficient to prove he was in control of the vehicle. We affirm.

Notice that the defendant has raised three issues for the court to address. Many judicial opinions address more than one issue. Often, only one of these issues will be relevant to your problem. You should carefully read the whole case, but you will focus your study of the case on the particular issue that concerns the problem at hand. In the Potter case, that issue is the meaning of "driving" under the New Hampshire statute.

CASE FILE 1: Assignment—Deconstructing a Case

In the *Holloran* case, identify the court, the parties, and the procedural history.

PRACTICAL TIP

In the appendix of your *Bluebook* under "United States Jurisdictions" you will find the citation form for every state. These pages will also indicate to you what the court system is in a particular state and what each level of the court is called.

---

c. Distinguishing Background Case Facts Versus Decisive Case Facts

In the *Winstead* case above, what follows is the court's rendition of the case facts. These paragraphs appear in the beginning of the court's opinion:

> The record supports the following facts. The charge arose out of an incident on April 6, 2002, when, at approximately 3:13 a.m., Officer Shawn L. Hallock of the Claremont Police Department discovered the defendant in a car in the Wal-Mart parking lot. The defendant was sleeping upright in the driver's seat, with the car engine running. At trial, the defendant testified that he decided to sleep in his car because he was "not…capable to drive anywhere," and that the car was running so he could stay warm. The defendant further testified that while he had no intention of driving the car, he did unlock the door, sit in the driver's seat, push the clutch in, move the gear selector to neutral, start the engine, and turn on the heater.
>
> Hallock approached the car and attempted to wake the defendant. When the defendant awoke and spoke with Hallock, Hallock "immediately smelled an odor of intoxicant." The defendant admitted to Hallock that he had consumed a six-pack of Bacardi Silvers that evening. Hallock asked the defendant to perform field sobriety tests, which the defendant failed. Hallock subsequently arrested the defendant for driving while intoxicated.
>
> After his arrest, the defendant was taken to the Claremont Police Department where he read and signed the Administrative License Suspension Form, which authorized the police to perform any combination of breath, blood, urine, or physical testing. The defendant was first given an intoxilyzer breath test, which resulted in a blood alcohol content (BAC) of 0.07. The result of the defendant's intoxilyzer test was below the statutorily defined level (BAC of 0.08) for *prima facie* evidence of intoxication. *See* RSA 265:82. Hallock then asked the defendant to take a blood test. The defendant testified that Hallock requested a blood test only for drugs. The defendant's blood was tested for both drugs and alcohol, *246 which resulted in a BAC of 0.08. The results of both tests were admitted at trial without objection. The district court found the defendant guilty and denied his motion to reconsider. This appeal followed.

The following excerpt is where the court identifies the critical facts on which they based their holding. This appears toward the end of the paragraph:

> Here, the defendant was also found asleep in the driver's seat of a car in a parking lot with the engine running. Moreover, the defendant testified at trial that he unlocked the door, sat in the driver's seat, pushed the clutch in, moved the gear selector to neutral, started the engine, and turned on the heater. Given these facts and the reasonable inferences therefrom, a rational trier of fact could find beyond a reasonable doubt that the defendant was in actual physical control of the car before he fell asleep. *See Willard,* 139 N.H. at 571, 660 A.2d 1086.

Notice that the court relies on only some of the facts to reach a conclusion about whether the defendant, Winstead, was in actual physical control of the car. How do you know this? The court says, "Given these facts and the reasonable inferences therefrom...." The "given" facts the court refers to are listed in the two sentences above (that the engine was running, that the defendant was in the front seat, etc.). These are the specific facts it uses to justify finding that the defendant was "driving." The court is signaling the reader that these are the facts that decided the defendant's status.

Why is it so important to know the *decisive* facts of the case? Because it will help you find the answer to your client's problem. Let's look at the facts of Potter's case. You have been asked to analyze whether he was "driving" under the New Hampshire law. The *Winstead* case tells you certain indicia of control showed that the defendant was "driving"—that the defendant was in the driver's seat, pushed in the clutch, moved the gear selector, and turned on the heater. In Potter's case, there are also indicia of control, though they may not be exactly the same ones. This tells you that these indicia of his control will likely be decisive in deciding whether he was "driving." Once you have identified the critical facts of the opinion (or opinions), you can identify the critical facts of your client's case.

The opinion will contain background that gives context to the case. In *Winstead,* an example of a background, or context, fact is that the incident occurred at 3:13 AM. The court does not mention this fact as contributing to its holding, but it gives the reader context for the case. If the case were a burglary instead of a DUI, the fact that the time was 3:13 AM would probably be a decisive fact. But in this case, the time does not affect the disposition. Similarly, the fact that the defendant read and signed an Administrative License Suspension Form is not pertinent to resolving the case.

Because courts often have to resolve more than one issue, particular facts may be decisive for one issue, but background facts for another issue. For example, in *Winstead,* the court' explains that the defendant's car was parked in a Wal-Mart parking lot. This fact is not relevant to the question of whether the defendant was driving, but it is relevant to the issue raised regarding equal protection:

> The defendant next argues that his right to equal protection was violated because Officer Hallock testified that he does not typically disturb people parked in recreational vehicles (RVs) in the Wal-Mart parking lot. Thus, the defendant argues, he was treated differently because he was in a car. We conclude, however, that this issue was also not preserved for appellate review.

CASE FILE 1: Assignment—Distinguish Background Versus Decisive Facts

Identify the background and the decisive facts of *O'Malley* and *Holloran*.

d. Identifying the Court's Reasoning (IRAC)

Most court opinions follow a structure. For each issue (and often courts are addressing more than one issue in an opinion), the opinion will begin by setting out the issue. Often, in conjunction with the issue, the court will set out a brief (one- or two-sentence) summary of the moving party's argument on the particular point.

This is typically followed by an explanation of the law that relates to the issue. Next the court applies the law, as it has explained it, to the facts of the case before it. Finally, the court will conclude with the outcome of the case. Sometimes a court will begin with the conclusion on the issue, and then repeat the conclusion after the explanation of the law and the application to the facts. This structure is referred to as "IRAC"—Issue, Rule, Application, and Conclusion. In various forms, the IRAC structure is the time-worn method of reasoning through a legal problem.

Although many opinions follow the IRAC structure and include the elements described above, they don't always follow the structure or include all of the IRAC elements. When you are studying a case, you may have to hunt for the elements.

Let's look at the court's reasoning in *Winstead*. Note that we will focus only on the part of the opinion that addresses the issue in our case—the meaning of "driving" under the New Hampshire statute.

[4] Finally, the defendant argues that because he was asleep, only turned on the heat and had no intent to drive the car, there was insufficient evidence for the trial court to find that he was in control of the car and thus operating a vehicle under the influence. We must determine "whether a rational trier of fact…could have found beyond a reasonable doubt that the defendant was in actual physical control of the **778 [vehicle]." _State v. Holloran_, 140 N.H. 563, 564-65, 669 A.2d 800 (1995) (per curiam); _see_ RSA 265:82; RSA 259:24 (1993).

This part of the opinion begins with a restatement of the defendant's argument, followed by the issue.

[5] "To have 'actual physical control' of a motor vehicle, one must have the capacity bodily to guide or exercise dominion over the vehicle at the present time." _State v. Willard_, 139 N.H. 568, 571, 660 A.2d 1086 (1995) (emphasis omitted). While a person who is sound asleep cannot have such a capacity, "circumstantial evidence which excludes any other rational conclusion is sufficient…to establish beyond a reasonable doubt the _actus reus_ set out in a motor vehicle statute." _Id._ (quotation omitted).

Here, the court is giving the overall **rule** on the meaning of "driving" in New Hampshire.

This case is indistinguishable from _Willard_. In _Willard_, the defendant was found asleep in the driver's seat of his vehicle in a parking lot with the vehicle's engine idling. A police officer woke him, determined he was intoxicated and arrested him for driving while intoxicated. In holding that *248 a rational trier of fact could find that the defendant was in _actual physical control_ of the vehicle, we noted that "if circumstantial evidence were to prove that [the] defendant [ ] started his car before falling asleep, he would have been in actual physical control of it while awake and in the driver's seat." _Id._; see also _Atknson v. State_, 331 Md. 199, 627 A.2d 1019, 1028 (1993) ("Indeed, once an individual has started the vehicle, he or she has come as close as possible to actually [operating it] without doing so and will generally be in 'actual physical control' of the vehicle.").

Next, the court further **explains the rule** by using **case illustrations**. Notice that the court first briefly describes the facts from Willard and then gives the holding and rationale for the holding.

Here, the defendant was also found asleep in the driver's seat of a car in a parking lot with the engine running. Moreover, the defendant testified at trial that he unlocked the door, sat in the driver's seat, pushed the clutch in, moved the gear selector to neutral, started the engine and turned on the heater. Given these facts and the reasonable inferences therefrom, a rational trier of fact could find beyond a reasonable doubt that the defendant was in actual physical control of the car before he fell asleep. _See Willard_ 139 N.H. at 571, 660 A.2d 1086.

Here the court has compared and **applied** the facts from Willard to the facts in Winstead.

In the same paragraph, the court gives its holding, or **conclusion**.

Affirmed.

IRAC is a very basic structure. You will use it in your own legal writing, but with some variation as the case you are working on dictates. Although the structure is very similar to a court opinion, because a lawyer has different goals than a judge, IRAC is usually a basic scaffold, but you may use it in a variety of ways. Lawyers often use a structure with the acronym CREAC. This stands for Conclusion, Rule, Explanation of the rule, Application of the rule, and Conclusion (yes, Conclusion is in there twice—more on this when we break down how to write an analysis). There are many variations of the acronym for legal writing structure, including TRAC (Thesis, Rule, Application, Conclusion), BaRac (Bold Assertion, Rule, Application, Conclusion), or CREXAC (Conclusion, Rule, Explanation of rule, Application, Conclusion). These are only a few and your particular writing professor may have one that's preferred as a teaching tool. Whatever specific structure you are directed to use, the purpose for using the structure and the general elements are similar.

To break it down, here is a more detailed way to imagine how the acronym IRAC actually works in the context of court opinions:

I: Issue: This can be either the overall issue that contains more than one issue, or the individual issue therein.

R: The rule section is broken down into the overall rule and the explanation of the rule with illustrations from the cases.

A: The application shows how the law applies to the case before the court.

C: The conclusion gives the holding.

CASE FILE 1 : Assignment—Identify How the O'Malley Opinion Uses the IRAC Structure

Label in the margins what each piece of the court's analysis is according to the IRAC structure.

e. Understanding How a Court Reasons

While IRAC is the structure a court typically uses to explain a decision, *how* it reaches a decision usually is based on one or several kinds of legal reasoning. Understanding how courts reason through a legal problem should help you reason through your own analysis. Lawyers, like judges, make different kinds of arguments and use different kinds of reasoning depending on the case. Four types of reasoning are summarized below. Note that there are more, and court opinions often contain a combination of two or more kinds of reasoning.

- *Reasoning based on precedent (akin to stare decisis).* A court will apply a rule to a set of facts to reach a conclusion by looking at prior cases with similar facts and recognizing how the rule was applied in the prior cases. The court will reach a similar conclusion because the facts of the prior cases are similar enough to warrant this outcome. To justify the conclusion the court will need to show *why* the prior cases' facts are similar. A good example of this kind of reasoning is in the cases you read for case file 1. Review the last two paragraphs of *Winstead.* The court explicitly compares the facts from *Willard,* noting that the two cases have almost "indistinguishable" facts. In the next paragraph, the court justifies its conclusion by demonstrating precisely how the two fact patterns are similar. This is how the court reasoned.

The prior case's facts may also be so different that a new outcome is warranted in the present case. For example, if there had been a prior New Hampshire case where the defendant was in the *passenger* seat asleep instead of in the driver's seat, the court would likely distinguish those facts, saying that they are so different from the facts of *Winstead,* where the defendant was in the driver's seat, that a different result is warranted. The court's reasoning in *Diaz* (page 34) also contains precedential reasoning. Notice how the court uses explicit comparisons to the cases it has described:

> Applying the above-mentioned principles and case law, we hold that the trial court correctly found as a matter of law that the defendants did not owe the plaintiffs a duty under the facts of this case. Unlike the cases cited by the parties, the crosswalk at the intersection in question was controlled by a "Don't Walk" signal. Nonetheless, the instant plaintiff chose to ignore it and proceed across the remainder of the intersection. Unlike *Sweet,* the plaintiff was not a youngster who relied on the directions of an adult. While we agree that *Sweet* is good law, we do not go as far as *Valdez* where it is implied that a duty would exist if the plaintiff interpreted the bus driver's gesture as something more than an indication that the driver would not move the bus until the plaintiff passed.

- *Reasoning based on interpretation.* Courts will also base a ruling on the language of a statute or regulation. This type of reasoning can be combined with precedent reasoning because often interpreting statutes requires defining particular words or phrases in statutes. Courts will look at past cases where the same or similar language has been interpreted. They will analyze the "plain meaning" and they may also review legislative history to discern the legislature's intent in writing the law. Sometimes courts will use the dictionary when interpreting the meaning of a word in a statute.

Here is an example of interpretative reasoning in a case where the defendant was arrested for DUI while riding a motorized stand-up two-wheel. The defendant, a healthy 25-year-old man who was using the scooter recreationally, unsuccessfully argued that the scooter was not a "vehicle" and even if it was, his use of the scooter should have fallen within a "mobility enhancement" exception of the statute. Note how the court discusses the words of the statute, the sentence structure of the statute, and the legislative history of the statute:

> Defendant contends there was insufficient evidence of a violation of N.C. Gen.Stat. §20–138.1 because the motorized scooter he was riding cannot be considered a "vehicle" within the meaning of the statute. We disagree.... "Statutory interpretation properly begins with an examination of the plain words of the statute." *Correll v. Division of Social Services*, 332 N.C. 141, 144, 418 S.E.2d 232, 235 (1992). If the language of a statute is clear, then the Court must implement the statute according to the plain meaning of its terms. *Id.* In the instant case, defendant was riding a motorized scooter with two wheels arranged in tandem, and the exclusionary provisions for horses, bicycles, and lawnmowers under N.C. Gen.Stat. §20–138.1(e) have no application. Defendant's scooter does meet the definition of a "device in, upon, or by which any person or property is or may be transported or drawn upon a highway" under N.C. Gen.Stat. §20–4.01(49).
>
> Defendant, nonetheless, argues that "mobility enhancement" should be construed broadly in light of the dearth of legal precedent concerning the definition of that term. We reject this construction for two reasons. First, although "mobility enhancement" is not specifically defined in the statute, its placement within the sentence discussing "mobility impairment" leads us to conclude that the two terms are closely related and contravenes ascribing the broad definition urged by defendant. Indeed, there is no evidence that defendant was using the scooter other than for strictly recreational purposes. Second, the exception for devices being used for "mobility enhancement" was added to the sentence concerning "mobility impairment" in 2001 as part of "An Act to Make Technical Corrections and Conforming Changes to the General Statutes as Recommended by the General Statutes Commission." *See* Act of Dec. 6, 2001, ch. 487, §51, 2001 N.C. Sess. Laws 2725, 2806 (codified at <u>N.C. Gen.Stat. §20–4.01</u>(49) (2003)). In a memorandum, the General Statutes Commission explained that "[t]his bill makes corrections of a *technical nature* to various sections of the General Statutes." Memorandum from the Gen. Statutes Comm'n to Sen. Fletcher L. Hartzell & Rep. Bill Culpepper, N.C. Gen. Assembly (Dec. 3, 2001)(on file with the North Carolina Supreme Court Library) (emphasis added). Therefore, adding the term "mobility enhancement" was a technical change that did not substantively expand the existing mobility impairment exception to the term "vehicle." (From *State v. Crow* 175 N.C.App. 119 (N.C. 2005))

- ***Rule-based reasoning.*** When a rule is indisputable and requires no interpretation, there is little reasoning to be done. For example, a law imposing a 55 miles per hour speed limit is a clear, objective standard. If your client was accused of driving at 80 miles per hour, there would be no need to argue about whether he violated the speed limit (if in fact he was going 80). Instead, you would give the rule (or law) and give no reasoning. If, instead, your client was charged with violating a law that prohibited driving at an unreasonable speed, you would need to analyze for your reader what "unreasonable"' means by doing precedential or other kinds of reasoning. In Dr. Potter's case, the rule that a driver must have .08 or higher blood alcohol concentration (BAC) to be over the legal limit is a clear standard. If Dr. Potter's BAC was .12, there would be little analysis regarding the law on this point, you would simply state the legal standard as a fact. If, instead, the law was that a person is prohibited from driving in an impaired condition, you would have to analyze and explain the meaning of "impaired" by doing precedential or other types of reasoning.

- *Reasoning based on policy.* A court may derive its holding from legal authority, but it may also justify a holding based on social policy or standards. Review the last paragraph of the *Diaz* decision on page 34 and reprinted below. The court says that the question of a signaler's duty concerns matters of "legal and social policies." The court is explicitly considering social norms in determining an answer in the case. Societal or economic concerns are another way a court justifies a case's outcome.

> We agree that an injury is foreseeable here. But whether a legal duty exists involves **1234 ***802 more than just foreseeability of possible harm; it also involves legal and social policies. (*Swett,* 169 Ill.App.3d 78, 119 Ill.Dec. 838, 523 N.E.2d 594.) Here, the magnitude of guarding against the injury and the consequence of placing that burden on the defendant weigh heavily in favor of finding no duty. An adult pedestrian with no obvious impairments should be held responsible for deciding whether gestures and directions given by a motorist can be safely followed. We simply do not believe that the instant bus driver's act of common courtesy should be transformed into a tort thereby giving the plaintiff license to proceed across an intersection against a warning light and without taking any precautions of her own.

Keep in mind that courts often start with rule-based, interpretive, or precedential reasoning rather than policy-based reasoning because a court's function is to decide the law (or rule).

f. Deconstructing and Synthesizing Case Law to Form a Rule for Your Client's Case

Once a lawyer believes that he or she has completed the research and gathered the legal authority needed to address the client's problem, the next step is pulling the decisive facts and rules from the cases to synthesize an overall rule. This is the rule or principle that will apply to the client's case and hopefully guide the lawyer toward a thoughtful prediction or a likely outcome.

A statute or regulation can form the basis of a rule that will guide a lawyer in solving a client's problem. However, interpreting the meaning of the statute and how the statute specifically should apply to a client requires going beyond the statute and will involve reading cases that address the statute.

In Dr. Potter's situation, the cases and the statute have already been researched so you do not need to do that part of the work. Now you need to figure out, based on the legal authority provided, if Dr. Potter was "driving" under the New Hampshire statute.

i. Synthesizing Rules from Cases

A legal problem will usually not be solved by a simple black and white answer, but it can happen. An example of a simple black and white answer would be if your client was 16 years old and had been arrested for DUI in New Hampshire. Let's say the client took a breathalyzer and registered a .04 and wanted to know if that violated the New Hampshire law. The answer is straightforward and can be easily answered by referring to the statute. The statute prohibits someone who is 21 or younger from driving with blood alcohol content greater than .02.

It is more likely that solving legal problems will involve complex research and analysis. The first step is to read and study the law. The next step is to put together the rules from the cases to form a guiding rule that can apply to your client's case. Remember that the rules can come from statutes (or regulations) and from cases. If there is no statute that applies, then the rule or rules will come from cases. In either situation, putting together slightly disparate principles to form one consolidated principle that applies to a client's problem is the next step.

Here is an example of synthesizing rules or principles:

Imagine that you live in a town where the state legislature has made it a criminal violation to walk on a public sidewalk while texting on a

mobile device. You have a client who was arrested after a police officer saw her tapping on her iPhone as she walked on a sidewalk. It turns out that she wasn't texting, but instead was looking at directions to where she was going on a MapQuest application. Has she violated the statute? At first glance, it seems not. She was not "texting" per se. But what if the definition of texting included in the law says that texting is any form of digital communication? There are three cases that have been brought to an appellate court that deal with this statute.

Case A upheld a conviction of a young man who was texting with a friend as he walked down the sidewalk. The court said that according to the plain meaning as defined in *Webster's Tenth New Int'l Dictionary 2584 (2012)*, "texting" means to communicate digitally with another by text messaging. Because the young man was engaged in a digital communication with another person, the court held he was "texting" and therefore it was a clear violation of the statute.

Case B reversed a conviction of a young woman who was playing an interactive game on her iPhone as she walked down the sidewalk. The court justified this by explaining that the law prohibited texting that amounts to interactive digital communication and because playing a game does not require communication with another, there was no violation. The underlying reason for the law is safety to citizens walking on the street.

Case C upheld a conviction of a man who was using a smartphone to write an e-mail to another person while he was walking down the sidewalk. The court reasoned that e-mailing fits within the definition of digital communication because it involves communicating with another person and the statute does not make an exception for communication that is not contemporaneous. The court in Case C reiterated the safety concerns inherent in distracted pedestrians engaged in digital communication with another individual.

How do we reconcile the statute and the three cases and apply them to our client's case?

First, look for the commonalities in the three cases. Here, the cases address pedestrians who are walking while doing something on their phones. But in the second case, the pedestrian is not communicating with another person, only playing a game.

Notice that in each case the common principle is that there is a statutory violation if the defendant's conduct on his or her phone *involves actual communication with another individual.*

Our client was not engaged in communication with another individual. She was using a resource on her phone to get directions. Therefore, you can predict that she likely did not violate the statute.

The synthesized rule could be:

> Under the state statute, it is a violation to text on a mobile device while walking on a public sidewalk. (cite to statute) The court has interpreted texting to require communication with another individual. (cite) Interacting with a smartphone in a manner that does not involve communication with another is not a violation. (cite to cases)

ii. Identifying the Court's Reasoning

When courts decide cases, often they will specifically explain *why* the decision is justified. The court in Case A, above, gives no reasoning for its decisions. Case B contains reasoning and Case C reaffirms it and does not add to it. Here, the justification for finding no violation in Case B is that an interactive game is less distracting (whether you agree with that or not!).

CASES	Case A	Case B	Case C	Commonalities
DECISIVE FACTS	D texting with a friend.	D playing a game on iPhone.	D e-mailing on a smartphone.	
RULE (holding)	Violation because D is engaged in digital communication with another.	No violation because D not engaged in interactive communication. Reasoning: it is more distracting to be in conversation with another, and a pedestrian who is communicating with another is less likely to look away and pay attention to what is happening on the street.	Violation because D engaged in communication with another even though it is not in live time. Reaffirmed reasoning from Case B.	Violation must involve with communication with another person, even even if not contemporaneous.

The synthesized rule together with the reasoning would look like this (the reasoning is italicized):

> Under the state statute, it is a violation to text on a mobile device while walking on a public sidewalk. The court has interpreted texting to require communication with another individual. Interacting with the smartphone in a manner that does not involve communication with another is not a violation *because it is less likely to be a distraction to a pedestrian.*

Based on this rule, our client's conduct does not seem to violate the statute.

Synthesizing the law and reconciling legal principles from a number of authorities is at the heart of what lawyers do. By studying relevant authorities carefully, a lawyer can interpret a body of law and apply it to a client's problem. How well you can predict or argue a solution to a client's problem will depend on how well you have understood and synthesized the relevant law.

An important note about synthesizing a rule: Sometimes there is not much synthesis needed. If several cases simply restate the same rule and then apply it to similar facts, you may not need to synthesize. Instead, you will just restate the rule that is repeated in each case. Although rules can be modified by courts as each new fact scenario comes before the court, this is not always the case. The outcome of a case can also lead to little change in the rule applied.

Finally, sometime you will need to infer the reasons for a court's decision because the reasoning is incomplete or inaccurate.

CASE FILE 1: Assignment—Synthesizing the Rule

1. Make a case chart of the three cases in the Potter case file similar to the chart above.

2. Write down a rule that addresses the meaning of "driving" under New Hampshire law. The rule should look like this:

> "A person is driving under the New Hampshire law even when seated in a stationary vehicle if _____."

g. Identifying Decisive Facts from a Client's Case

The rule that you construct from the legal authority in the Potter case will help to distinguish the decisive facts of your client's case. Remember that in a court's opinion there are background facts and decisive facts. The same is true of your client's case. To identify the decisive facts, you have to first study the law and figure out what the rules and decisive facts were from the cases. Once you know this information, you will be able to identify the decisive facts from your client's case. Decisive facts are legally significant facts that will affect the outcome of the case.

In the cases used for the synthesis example above (Cases A, B, and C), a legally significant fact of our client's case is that she was engaged in looking at directions on her phone, not communicating with another individual. If the facts of our client's case had included that it was a sunny day, or that the client was a tourist from Europe, these facts would not affect the outcome of the case. The synthesized rule we came up with from Cases A, B, and C helped us understand that the critical fact that led to the court's decisions involved whether the defendant was in communication with another.

The fact that our client is looking at directions and not communicating with another leads to a probable outcome. She likely wasn't violating the statute. Thus, if the client came to us for advice, such as asking whether she should plead guilty or go to trial to fight the charge, we would advise that she likely has a good argument that she wasn't violating the statute and therefore may want to fight the charge.

Let's turn to Potter's case. From the three cases, you know that the court's decisions all turn on indicia of a defendant's control over a car. To identify

CASES	Case A	Case B	Case C	Commonalities	Decisive Client Facts
DECISIVE FACTS	D texting with a friend.	D playing a game on iPhone.	D e-mailing on a smartphone.		Client looking up directions on MapQuest App
RULE (holding)	Violation because D is engaged in digital communication with another.	No violation because D not engaged in interactive communication.	Violation because D engaged in communication with another even though it is not in live time.	Violation must involve communication with another person, even if not contemporaneous.	

the decisive facts from Potter's case, look for whether there are any indicia of his control over the car.

CASE FILE 1: Assignment—Identifying Decisive Client Facts

1. Make a list of the decisive facts from Potter's case.
2. Can you predict from this list whether he is likely in violation of the statute?
3. What if Potter had been discovered asleep in the back seat of the car? Would the list be different? Would the prediction be different?

CHAPTER 6

The Office Memorandum: Components

The office memorandum format is fundamental to legal writing. Its mission is to educate the reader about the issue, the facts, the likely arguments on both sides, and sometimes, next steps. The format is also frequently the basis of an e-mail or a client letter. The over-arching mission is always the same—to educate the reader about the issue. You will learn how to write an office memorandum beginning with your first "client" problem described in Case File 1. Each of the successive case files will require you to write increasingly more complex office memorandums.

Once you understand the rule (or rules) that will apply to your case and you have identified the decisive facts from your own case, the next step is to put pen to paper. For Potter's case, you are asked to write the discussion section of an objective memorandum. Case files 2 and 3 require that you write an entire memorandum. This type of memorandum is typically written "in house;" that is, as an interoffice communication. You might be asked to put the information in an e-mail or hard copy. Either way, there is a basic format to follow that is universal in the legal profession. What follows is a brief introduction to the parts of a legal memorandum. In Chapter 7 you will learn how to draft the parts.

A. PARTS OF AN INTEROFFICE LEGAL MEMORANDUM

The parts of a typical interoffice memorandum include:

- Heading
- Issue or Question Presented
- Brief Answer or Summary
- Facts
- Discussion
- Conclusion

Each part of an office memorandum has a distinct function. These will be explained below and examples will be given for each part. The parts are identified below in the sample memorandum from page 9.

INTER-OFFICE MEMORANDUM

Heading

To: Attorney Supervisor

From: Student Lawyer

Date: September 15, 2011

Re: ***State v. Albert*: Relevance of Albert's prior shoplifting**

Issue

Issue (also can be called Question Presented)

In Maureen Albert's trial for theft of a ham from a Hannaford Supermarket (Hannaford), is evidence of a prior incident relevant where in the prior case Albert removed a turkey from the same Hannaford without paying?

Brief Answer

Brief Answer (also called Summary) Note there are no case cites here.

Probably yes. Evidence of Albert's earlier shoplifting incident is probably relevant under New Hampshire Rule of Evidence 404(b). Admission of prior bad act evidence under Rule 404(b) requires that: (1) the evidence is relevant for a purpose other than showing the defendant's character, (2) there is clear proof that the defendant actually committed the prior act, and (3) the probative value of the evidence outweighs its prejudicial impact. As instructed, this memo addresses only the question of relevance. Albert has made her intent an issue by specifically claiming she removed the ham accidentally. The evidence of Albert's prior shoplifting is thus likely relevant to rebut her claim that she took the ham by accident.

Facts

Facts — these are the facts of your client's case. Notice that there is no law cited here. Only facts from your record or file.

In November 2009, three months before the current incident occurred, Maureen Albert left the Hannaford's in Concord, New Hampshire, without paying for a turkey that she had placed in the bottom of her cart. Albert returned the turkey, was warned about her behavior, and was not prosecuted.

In February 2010, Albert took a cart containing a spiral ham out of the same Hannaford's without paying for it. When a Hannaford's employee stopped her in the parking lot, Albert said that she left the store because she realized she had forgotten her wallet in her car. She stated that she did not intend to steal the ham and had removed it from the store accidentally.

The State has charged Albert with shoplifting for the second incident. In her trial, the State wants to introduce evidence of the turkey incident to prove that she intended to steal the ham.

Discussion

Discussion — The legal analysis that supports your prediction(s). The first paragraph is an introduction or roadmap of the analysis.

Albert's prior act involving the turkey is relevant for a purpose other than character because she raised the issue of intent, and the prior act is factually similar and close in time to the charged act. Evidence is relevant for a purpose other than character if it (1) has a direct bearing on an issue actually in dispute, and (2) a clear and logical connection exists between that act and the crime charged. *McGlew*, 658 A.2d at 1194. The trial court must make specific findings on each of these elements. *Id.*

1. Direct Bearing on Issue in Dispute

[text omitted]

Subheadings — These are headings that divide the analysis by sub-issues.

2. Clear and Logical Connection

[text omitted]

1. The Heading

The purpose of a heading in a legal memorandum (or "legal memo") is self-evident: it identifies the recipient, author, and date. The reference (Re:) line should clearly identify the client file (sometimes by a number) and the specific issue being addressed. The best practice is to be as specific as possible. Interoffice memoranda become a part of a client's file and can be resources for later research or preparation for a deposition, client meeting, trial, or appeal. Office memoranda might also be used by lawyers who are researching the same issue but for a different client. Thus, being clear in the reference (Re:) line is essential. If this line only contained "Albert Trial Issue," for example, a later reader would have to search the document to find out what the specific issue was. How you label documents is actually of critical importance. This is also true for how you save memoranda in a computer file. You want to be able to easily access the memorandum not just by client name but also by subject matter.

EXAMPLE A: Correct heading

To:	Sally Lawyer
From:	Lester Associate
Date:	September 10, 2013
Re:	Robert Reno; # 55-211167; Contract – 2010 Employment Contract-Enforceability of Non-Compete Clause

EXAMPLE B: Incorrect heading

To:	Sally Lawyer
From:	Lester Associate
Date:	September 10, 2013
Re:	Robert Reno file

Notice that the specificity of **Example A** will be more easily identifiable and enduring.

2. The Issue or Question Presented

In Chapter 7 you will learn specifically how to write an issue statement. The terms "issue" and "question presented" are interchangeable in a legal memorandum. Typically, this is a matter of personal stylistic preference. This part of the memorandum identifies the exact question you have been asked to analyze. The form of the question will vary depending on the type of analysis you are doing.

For example, if, as in the example on page 13 where the question relates only to a specific law, absent a client's particular facts, then the issue will only contain the law:

Issue
What steps are required to initiate and carry out eviction proceedings for a tenant who has not paid rent?

If the issue relates to a particular client's legal problem, then the question presented will contain decisive facts as well as the legal question:

Issue

In Maureen Albert's trial for theft of a ham from a Hannaford Supermarket (Hannaford), is evidence of a prior incident relevant where in the prior case Albert removed a turkey from the same Hannaford without paying?

Many different kinds of legal documents begin with an issue. Memoranda or briefs to courts begin with some form of an issue. Interoffice memoranda always begin with an issue in some form. There are a number of different ways to write an issue. In the section below you will find two of these, but when you are writing one in practice you may encounter supervisors who prefer that the issue be written in a certain way. These instructions should give you a sufficient base that can be easily amended to suit different styles. Notice that the issue here contains three parts:

- First, there are facts that orient the reader to the context for the question: "In Maureen Albert's trial for theft of a ham from a Hannaford Supermarket (Hannaford)." Sometimes these context facts will take more than just a phrase followed by a comma to explain. The context facts could be a sentence, or even two sentences, depending on how complicated the case is.
- Next, is the legal issue: "is evidence of a prior incident relevant…" Admissibility is the legal question in the case.
- Finally, a statement of the key, decisive facts: "where in the prior case Albert removed a turkey from the same Hannaford without paying?" The removal of a turkey from the same store is a key, decisive fact.

The format of an issue looks like this:

[Context facts – your client's decisive facts] "is" [legal issue] "where" [key, decisive facts]

The order of these elements can vary. The words can also vary. For example, "is" can be preplaced with "does," "can," or another similar word. "Where" can be replaced with "when," "if," or another similar word.

The issue can also start with "Whether." For example:

Whether looking at directions on a smartphone on a public sidewalk constitutes "communication" with another in violation of a statute prohibiting Texting While Walking.

This form can also be personal to a particular client:

Whether Jane Carter's conduct of walking on a public sidewalk looking at MapQuest directions on a smartphone constituted "communication" with another in violation of the statute prohibiting Texting While Walking.

An issue can be quite short or it can contain two or more sentences.

> ### PRACTICAL TIP
>
> Write a draft of your issue before you begin your research. Revise the issue after your research is complete. Revise it again after you finish writing the whole discussion section. You want to begin with a question that orients you to the issue at hand so that you are reminded not to go off on a tangent. As you become more of an expert in the particular legal question you are analyzing you will be better able to draft a specific and effective issue.

EXAMPLE: A short issue

Does Lilyview Hospital have a duty to Susan Stanford <u>for negligent infliction of emotional distress</u> where Stanford went into shock after observing medical personnel attempting to revive her son after an anesthesia alarm accidentally malfunctioned?

Legal issue
Decisive facts

EXAMPLE: A longer issue containing several sentences

Susan Stanford went into shock while witnessing her son go into cardiac arrest as he recovered from routine hernia surgery. Hospital personnel had to revive Stanford's son after an anesthesia pump alarm accidentally failed, allowing him to receive an overdose of intervenous morphine. <u>Does Lilyview Hospital have a duty to Stanford for injuries resulting from this incident?</u>

Decisive facts

Legal issue

Both of the issues above contain the two necessary components. The legal issue and the decisive facts.

Although there are many correct ways to write an issue, there are also things to avoid:

1. Do not include excess information that distracts or obscures the point.

   EXAMPLE: An issue with too much information

   Daniel Stanford, an 18 year old, underwent routine hernia surgery at Lilyview Hospital on February 2, 2012. As he was recovering, he was hooked up to a morphine pump to control pain. His mother, Susan Stanford, sat by his bed and witnessed her son's lips turn blue and his breathing stop as a loud beeping came from the pump. Stanford now experiences headaches and insomnia from the shock of the incident. Is Lilyview liable to Stanford for these injuries?

2. Do not skimp on critical information.
3. Avoid being too general in an issue. Your goal is to identify the *precise* combined factual and legal question that you are analyzing.

   EXAMPLES: Issues that are too general

   What constitutes "texting" under the state statute prohibiting "Texting While Walking"?

Is Lilyview Hospital liable to Susan Stanford for negligent infliction of emotional distress?

These questions do not identify either the precise legal issue or the decisive facts.

a. How to Draft a Short Issue

One way to draft an issue is to use a template:[1]

Inquiry Word	Decisive Legal Question	Connecting Words	Decisive Facts
Does [Is/Can/Did]	Lilyview Hospital have a duty to Stanford for negligent infliction of emotional distress	Where [when/if]	Stanford went into shock after observing medical personnel attempting to revive her son after an anesthesia alarm accidentally malfunctioned?

EXAMPLE:

Inquiry word
Connecting word

Decisive facts

In Maureen Albert's trial for theft of a ham from a Hannaford Supermarket (Hannaford), is evidence of a prior incident relevant where in the prior case Albert removed a turkey from the same Hannaford without paying?

Decisive legal question

b. How to Draft a Longer Issue

This version of an issue contains two to three sentences that give the decisive facts in a narrative fashion. These factual sentences are followed by the legal question.

To write this version of an issue you will need to know the decisive facts. Remember that these are the facts upon which your conclusion turns. If any one of these facts changed, the answer to the issue would be different. You will also need to know the precise legal question.

EXAMPLE:

Maureen Albert was arrested for shoplifting a ham from a supermarket on February 24, 2009. In November 2010, Albert was arrested after she left the same store without paying for a turkey. Is the November 2009 incident relevant in the current shoplifting case against Albert under N.H. R. Evid. 404(b)?

The first two sentences contain the decisive facts. The last sentence asks the specific legal question.

3. The Brief Answer or Summary

The brief answer or summary answers the issue and gives a quick description justifying the answer. The purpose is to tell the reader up front

---

1. Adapted from Coughlin, *A Lawyer Writes.*

what the memorandum is about. A busy legal reader (and most legal readers are busy) may only look at the summary of the memorandum at first in order to get a quick idea of where the case is going. The summary should be precise, clear, and short.

> **PRACTICAL TIP**
>
> Once you are working in a legal office, ask to see some sample interoffice legal memoranda. These will give you an idea of what the customs and expectations are with regard to style and format. In particular, you can find out what type of issues (or questions presented) and summaries (or brief answers) the office uses.

The brief answer begins with a "yes" or "no" that is a quick answer to the issue. The next sentence or sentences give the conclusion. This is followed by several sentences that summarize the reason for the conclusion.

The components of an effective summary are:

- A quick answer. This can be "yes" or "no." Or, if your conclusion is less certain, the quick answer can reflect that. It's acceptable to say "probably yes" or "probably no."
- A summary of the rule or rules upon which your conclusion is grounded.
- A short application of the facts to the legal rule or rules.
- An alert to reader of issues or sub-elements not being addressed.

The summary should not include any citations, nor should it include background information. Being concise is never more important than in the summary.

EXAMPLE: An ineffective summary

New Hampshire's test for duty turns on whether a victim contemporaneously perceives the negligent act. To determine if a defendant is liable the plaintiff must prove that: a) the injury was foreseeable; b) the defendant was at fault; c) the accident caused the injury; and d) expert testimony exists that proves plaintiff's physical symptoms. Lilyview Hospital was liable to Susan Stanford because she witnessed her son's cardiac arrest after his hernia surgery.

No specific answer given

Legal rule does not address specific issue of plaintiff's contemporaneous perception

No clear application of client's facts

EXAMPLE: Edited to improve effectiveness

Lilyview Hospital likely had a duty to Susan Stanford because her injuries were foreseeable and should have been prevented. The evidence is sufficient to prove the three elements of New Hampshire's foreseeability test for duty because: (1) Sanford was the mother of the initial victim, (2) she was close in proximity to the victim at the time of the accident, and (3) she contemporaneously perceived the accident when she heard the loud beep and saw her son in cardiac arrest. Since the hospital has conceded its breach caused Stanford's injury, only the duty question will be answered here.

Quick answer

Rule together with a brief application of client facts

Alert of what is not addressed

4. The Facts

The facts section explains the background and decisive facts that lead to the legal problem. For an interoffice memorandum, the facts can be from client or witness interviews, depositions, transcripts, police reports, or any other documents that form the basis of the legal problem. This section contains no legal analysis. It can be organized chronologically or by topic if there is more than one issue in the case. The facts should read like a story, pulling the reader through the narrative of what happened in an easily readable format. If the facts are complex, subheadings are helpful and reader-friendly.

PRACTICAL TIP

As with the issue, it is a good idea to write a draft of the summary first and then redraft when you have completed your legal analysis. This section should be the last thing that you write.

It may seem odd to draft the facts section after you have a draft of the issue, summary, and discussion sections. The logic in this order is that you won't know which facts matter until you have a true grasp on the legal analysis. Once you understand the law you will know which are the critical facts of your client's case—the ones that, if they were slightly different, could affect the outcome. For example, in the case involving the client accused of texting while walking, we know that what she was doing on her phone (looking at directions) is critical to the outcome of her case. The facts section of a memorandum about the texting client would need to include that detail.

Thus, the first step involves identifying the critical facts. The next step is to identify the background facts that give context to the case. For example, in the Potter case, it may not be a critical fact that he went to a bar after a difficult work day, but it helps to give the reader a picture of the event. Knowing why he was drinking gives context to facts. Think about how you can paint a vivid picture of what happened. Once you have a list of background facts, make an outline that organizes the facts either chronologically or by some other logic. Remember that you want your reader to get a good sense of the players in your case.

Any adverse facts must be included. Your analysis will address the adverse facts, most likely in your counter-analysis (see Chapter 13). Don't be afraid to acknowledge these.

Include procedural facts if the reader needs them to give context to the case. Here is an example of procedural facts from the sample memorandum on page 9:

The State has charged Albert with shoplifting for the second incident. In her trial, the State wants to introduce evidence of the turkey incident to prove that she intended to steal the ham.

Here are the steps to take in drafting the facts section:

1. Make a list of the critical facts.
2. Identify the background facts.
3. Outline the order in which you will describe the facts.
4. Draft the facts.
5. Cross check the facts in your discussion section to ensure you have mentioned every critical fact. Do not refer to a fact in the discussion section without putting it in the facts section.
6. If your facts are long (more than three pages), consider using sub-headings.
7. Make sure that your facts tell a story. The facts should not sound like a list.
8. Revise.

PRACTICAL TIP

You may need to give citation references to the facts in a legal memo. This will depend on the type of memo you are drafting and a law office's customary practice. Sometimes office memos include a cite after every sentence in the facts. Ask to see sample memos or ask whether the facts should include citations. The *Bluebook* includes instruction for how to cite documents.

---

5. The Discussion Section

The discussion section of the memorandum contains the legal analysis. This is where the law that guides your answer is explained and then applied to your client's facts. If this were a math problem, this would be where you "show your work." The discussion section serves to justify the conclusion or prediction you are making about the likely outcome of the case.

Perhaps more than any other part of the legal memorandum, the discussion section usually follows a set structure. Remember the reference to CREAC in Chapter 5? This structure and its purpose will be explained in detail in Chapter 7. For now, take a look at the discussion section of the interoffice memorandum on page 9. Notice that it begins with a brief introduction or roadmap. This is followed by two different sections, each with its own heading. These subsections first explain the law on the subpoint and then they apply the law on the subpoint to your client's facts. They begin the section with a sentence that gives the reader a conclusion about the paragraph's point.

The discussion section is the most complex part of the memorandum and the heart of the memorandum, which is why Chapter 7 is devoted entirely to this section of the memorandum.

6. The Conclusion

a. A Timeline for Writing and Interoffice Memorandum (after your research is done)

Most interoffice memoranda will end with a brief conclusion. Usually this section sums up the analysis and is almost a mirror of the brief answer.

Draft an issue. This will likely change and be revised as you proceed in the writing process, but it's a good idea to start by writing down what the question is that you must answer. Be specific here. Remember our client who was arrested for typing on her iPhone on a street? At the outset, you could formulate an issue such as: *Does searching for directions on an iPhone while on a public street violate the "No Texting" statute?* You may revise this, but at the outset it will help you stay focused on what you need to address.

Draft the discussion section. It may seem strange and out of order to write the discussion before the summary and the facts, however, the discussion section contains your legal analysis. You will need to know what is contained in your analysis before drafting the summary and the facts. Knowing the decisive facts for your case will depend on what the decisive facts were in the cases you will use. Thus, it's better to wait until you know and understand the law before drafting the facts.

Draft the facts. After you have a good idea about what you will say in the discussion, draft the facts section. Why? You won't know what facts will be decisive until you fully understand the legal analysis.

Draft the brief answer or summary. This is the last section to write. Because you will have to synthesize the law and facts into a clear and concise summary, it's impossible to get this right before you have an understanding of your analysis.

CHAPTER 7

Writing the Discussion Section of an Interoffice Memorandum

Writing the discussion section of a memorandum is a multi-step process, as outlined here:

1. *Identify the legal issue.* This comes after you have a good understanding of the client's facts and the problem the client has come to you for help with. Remember, as you develop your analysis, the issue will be refined.

2. *Research the law.* Once you identify the issue, look for the law that will address the question. Often, this process will start with reading a secondary source, which will give you an overview of the relevant law.

3. *Study the law.* This is where you read and re-read cases and statutes. As you do this, you will begin to focus in more on what will determine the outcome of your client's problem.

4. *Organize the information you have read.* In any given case you will probably have a number of legal authorities that together provide an answer to your client's problem. In the next section you are given a sample of one way to organize the authorities, but it is not the only way. Ultimately, you will develop a system of organization that suits the way you think and work.

5. *Synthesize the rule.* Once you have winnowed down the authorities, you need to sketch the rule that will apply to your client's case. Remember, this is what we did on page 68 where we put together the statute and cases on texting on a public way.

6. *Make an outline of your legal analysis.* Every legal analysis should begin with an outline or a roadmap so you know how the pieces of the analysis fit together and how you will structure the analysis on the page. One suggestion for an outline format will be made here, but ultimately, you will develop a style of outlining that works for you.

7. ***Write a draft of the analysis.*** This is where you will use some version of the CREAC structure discussed in Chapter 5.
8. ***Revise the draft.***
9. ***Revise the draft again as needed.***
10. ***Proofread and line edit.***

We have already addressed steps 1 through 3 and step 5. You will learn about doing research separately. We will now look at steps 4 and 6.

A. HOW TO ORGANIZE THE INFORMATION

One way to organize a number of authorities is to use a chart. It can help to see the commonalities in the cases if you lay out visually the important aspects of each case. The chart on page 70 is one example of how to organize authorities. It could be expanded to include other columns, depending on the case and your personal preferences.

For example, in the Potter case, assume that you have to research each of the elements of DUI: (1) driving, (2) on a way, (3) while under the influence. A chart might look like this:

Element	*Winstead*	*O' Malley*	*Holloran*	Synthesized Rule on Element
"Driving"	Decisive facts: Holding/Reasoning:	Decisive facts: Holding/Reasoning:	Decisive facts: Holding/Reasoning:	
"On a way"	Decisive facts: Holding/Reasoning:	Decisive facts: Holding/Reasoning:	Decisive facts: Holding/Reasoning:	
"Under the influence"	Decisive facts: Holding/Reasoning:	Decisive facts: Holding/Reasoning:	Decisive facts: Holding/Reasoning:	

You will also want to develop a way to keep track of the cases. Avoid having to leaf through each case to remind yourself of what it was about. Although you will continually go back to the cases, it's a good idea to have a form that you use to brief each case, or a 5 x 7 card for each case. The card system allows you to quickly pull out a case and see what the facts and holding were.

1. Make an Outline[1]

Often students arrive in law school unaccustomed to making an outline. In legal writing this step is critical because it forces you to think through the concepts clearly before you put pen to paper to start writing a draft. The outlining process begins during your research. You can tinker with the outline as your research progresses. Outlining will move you from analysis to writing.

When you start outlining you will probably be lost in a welter of concepts, facts, law, and reasoning. When you finish a complete outline, you will understand the analysis and have a logical, linear roadmap, that directs you through the issues, sub-issues, rules, cases, facts, and counter-arguments to the conclusion. Then you can write efficiently.

One caveat here: for some, writing an outline is not the way to begin the process.[2] You may need to get words on a page first, what Annie La-mott refers to as the "down draft."[3] If you fit that description, try making a very skeletal outline first so you have some idea of where you are going, then go ahead and write. *But* after you finish the "down draft," you'll need to organize what you wrote. You may find that after you have downloaded your ideas on paper, you are better able to see and understand a clear structure. The danger in this method is that when you finish the down draft and think you are done. This is very unlikely to be the case. Think of this stage as prewriting or a "brain dump" followed by putting the text in logical order.

Outlining serves several purposes:

- Puts ideas into linear structure.
- Shows relationships between ideas; for example, which is the overarching point and which are subordinate points.
- Helps you figure out where ideas belong logically.
- Enables you to remember all the different points and nuances of an analysis.
- Can show you what you understand and where you need more thought and/or research.
- If you do not understand a discussion/argument well enough to outline it, you do not understand it well enough to write it.
- If you do not outline, you are guaranteed to waste time reorganizing and rewriting. In addition, you will probably forget to include important details.

---

1. The information on outlining is derived from materials by Alice Briggs, the former Writing Specialist at UNH Law.
2. See Robbins, Johansen, Chestek, *Your Client's Story*, p. 116.
3. See Lamott, Annie, *Bird by Bird*, p. 25.

2. Format

- There is no "winning" formula for the way you format an outline. It is entirely personal and should work for you.
- At a minimum, the format must distinguish between overarching points and subordinate points. Frequently ordinals (I, A, 1, a, etc.) are used to accomplish this. In other words, using bullets that simply list the points will probably not be helpful.

3. Process

- Every writer develops a personal process for outlining. There is no one right way, provided the final outline is complete and useful, and the process for getting there is efficient.
- Do not be afraid to make several outlines. This can help you learn the analysis and enables you to explore different organizations to see which works best.
- Outlining can be done in phases or iterations, as discussed below, as your understanding of the analysis develops.
- Some writers begin with all the points they want to make and organize those (bottom-up outlining); other writers begin with the major points they want to make and then add the details (top-down outlining). Many writers use a combination of these approaches.

B. A STEP-BY-STEP APPROACH TO MAKING AN OUTLINE

Step 1. Identify the major steps or ideas in the analysis.
- Frequently, this will mean identifying the rule and its elements or factors.
- For example, if the topic is "when is a prior incident admissible in a defendant's criminal trial?" the rule would have three elements: (1) the evidence must be relevant for a purpose other than showing the defendant's character, (2) there must be clear proof that the defendant committed the act, and (3) the probative value must outweigh the prejudicial impact.
- You figure out the elements of a rule by looking at how the courts approach the rule. What topics do the courts discuss? What conclusions does a court draw in reaching its holding?
- You must synthesize cases and put together a rule that incorporates new aspects to the rule that the court has added. Remember Cases A, B, and C on page 70. Case C added an aspect to the rule (communication with another does not have to be live), and this should be included in the rule.

Step 2. Begin with a roadmap/global section.
- This is where you put all the information that the reader needs to understand the rest of the discussion/analysis.
  - If a piece of information is relevant to just one element, then it probably does not belong in the roadmap section.
  - If, however, a piece of information is relevant to the entire discussion/analysis, then it belongs in the roadmap section.
- Things to consider putting in the roadmap section include:
  - The answer to the question you've been asked.
  - The roadmap or overall rule.
  - Any interpretive standards that courts use when applying the rule. For example, do courts interpret the rule broadly or narrowly? Do courts apply the rule frequently or infrequently?
  - Any policy or purpose behind the rule.
  - Who carries the burden.
  - The relationships between elements or factors in the rule.
  - Any "givens"; that is, things that are already established or that you are not going to discuss.

Step 3. Make a section for each major step/idea/element.
- You may find as you proceed that you can combine two elements into one section, but separating them into separate sections is a good way to begin.
- Ask yourself whether each major idea/element needs to be broken down into sub-elements.
  - For example, the relevance element of the New Hampshire rule on admissibility of a prior incident can be broken down into subparts (direct bearing on an issue actually in dispute, and a clear and logical connection between the prior act and the current charge). The clear and logical connection is also broken into two subparts (prior incident is factually similar and close in time).

Step 4. Put the sections into a logical sequence.
- To determine the logical sequence, first decide whether the courts typically employ a certain sequence.
- If the courts do not use a particular sequence, then ask yourself whether logic compels a certain sequence. For example, does one element depend on another? In this case the dependent element must come after the primary element.
- If neither the courts nor logic dictates a sequence, start with the strongest element or the element that is most important to the client; put the second strongest/most important element last; and put any other elements in between in descending order of importance.

> **NOTE**
> **The next steps require going back to flesh out the outline and should be done for each section and sub-section of the outline.** You may choose to complete one section before beginning another, or you may decide to put rules in all the sections before moving to the next step.

Step 5. Write out the rules.
- Here you want to draft the rules and sub-rules.

Step 6. Indicate which case(s) you will use to illustrate/support/prove each point you need to make about the rule.
- Generally using more than one case is preferable.
- Consider using cases that show different aspects of the rule.
- Provide some citation information. These do not need to be full *Bluebook* cites; a case name and a pincite or even just a case name is sufficient. Including cites keeps you from making up propositions that you can't support. It is also a useful tool when you are writing from the outline.

Step 7. Identify which case(s) you are going to analogize to/distinguish from the client's facts.

Step 8. Make a list of all the points that might be relevant to this discussion/argument that you have not included in the outline.
- These may be points about the law or about the facts.
- Think about each point in the context of the outline and insert it where it makes logical sense.

Step 9. Write a conclusion for each section.
- You may change this conclusion as your analysis develops.

Step 10. Check for completeness.
- At this point, stop and consider whether the rule and the cases supporting it will support all the points/arguments you want to make about your client's facts.
- If you want to make a point/argument but the rule explanation doesn't support it, then you need to expand the rule explanation.

EXAMPLE: Outline of Albert Memorandum Discussion Section: Roadmap Paragraph and Relevance

    I. Roadmap: Prior Act Evidence Admissibility
       A. Evidence is likely admissible because A:
          1. Claims accident
          2. 2 acts (ham/turkey) are similar

      3. Witnesses offer clear proof A. acted

      4. High probative value/low prejudicial value

   B. Rule 404(b) allows prior act evidence if:

      1. Relevant for purpose other than D's character

      2. Clear proof exists D committed acts

      3. Probative value outweighs possible prejudice to D

   C. State has burden. *McGlew* @ 1193.

   D. 404(b) purpose is trial on merits, not character. *Bassett* @ 893.

  II. Relevance: Direct Bearing on Issue in Dispute Explained

   A. Turkey incident is relevant

   B. Evidence relevant if it has direct bearing on issue in dispute.

   C. *McGlew* @ 1194.

      1. Evidence has a direct bearing if to show absence of accident

         a. *Lesnick* admits prior act b/c D (wife) claimed stabbing of husband was accident in charged crime and prior act. @690.

         b. *Blackey* excludes evidence because D did not claim accident. @1334.

 III. Relevance: Direct Bearing on Issue in Dispute Applied to Albert's case

      2. Turkey has a direct bearing on whether Albert shoplifted.

         a. As *Lesnick* wife claimed 2 stabbings accidental, A claims both meat incidents accidental.

         b. Unlike *Blackey* D, A has claimed accident.

         c. (conclusion) Ct will find A's claim of accident puts her intent at issue by claiming accident.

 IV. Relevance: Clear and Logical Connection Explained

      3. Clear logical connection where factually similar, close in time

         a. Precise chain of reasoning must be articulated.

            i. *Lesnick* same weapon, victim, circumstances and few months apart, so prosecution could "articulate precise chain of reasoning" @ 690.

         b. Acts must be factually similar.

            i. *McGlew* no connection because different victim age, gender, and 6 years span between incidents, so not "clear and logical" that intent was the same @ 1194.

  V. Clear and Logical Connection: Applied to Albert's Case

      4. Turkey has a clear and logical connection to the charged crime

         a. Same type of product, similar removal from store, close in time; compare *Lesnick*.

         b. Unlike *McGlew* where State could not articulate precise chain of reasoning because facts too different.

         c. (conclusion) Ct. likely find "clear and logical" connection because of similarities.

 VI. Turkey Incident Meets 404(b) Relevance Requirement

CASE FILE 1: Assignment—Outlining

Write out an outline of the discussion section of the Potter memorandum.

C. EXPLAINING THE LAW IN A DISCUSSION

Remember, in legal writing we use structure. When you are writing a legal analysis of an issue, first you give the explanation of the law and then the application of the law to your client's facts. The structure is not hard and fast and will vary depending on what your client's problem is and what you are explaining and applying.

Explaining the law to the reader requires first beginning with the overall synthesized rule. Next, you explain more specifically how the rule works. If the rule is based on a statute, then the explanation may focus on further defining terms or construction. To do this, you may have to explain cases where the court defines and applies the term to specific situations. Our analysis of whether Dr. Potter was "driving" fits within this example.

If there is no statute that applies to the client's problem, the issue you are addressing may only involve explaining a rule that is based on common law cases. Or, you may be dealing with a statute where further explanation really isn't necessary. For example, in Dr. Potter's case, we could be asked to find the law on what the legal limits are on blood alcohol in New Hampshire. There is a clear-cut answer on this and thus no analysis would be necessary.

The challenge of writing about the law is that you will need to take what can be complex concepts and explain them in simple, understandable language. Whether you are explaining the law to a client, a colleague, or a judge, you must always use plain English and strive for simple, accurate descriptions of the law.

Case file 1 gives you the chance to explain the law using a statute and three cases. You have already laid the groundwork for this by studying the statute and the cases, briefing the cases, synthesizing the rule, and outlining the analysis.

In this chapter, you will learn an approach to explaining the law. On page 95, you will learn how to apply the specific law to your client's case.

1. The Roadmap (AKA Global) Paragraph

At the beginning of a legal discussion, you will give the reader an overall roadmap of the analysis that is to come. Other terms for describing this paragraph are the "global paragraph" or the "rule(s) paragraph." Here, we will refer to it as the roadmap paragraph. If the reader had only a few minutes and wanted to quickly understand your conclusion on the issue, he or she would be able to do so just by reading your roadmap paragraph. Once the reader had more time, he or she could come back and read the remainder of the discussion.

Remember, in legal writing conclusions come first. A roadmap paragraph should begin with your overall conclusion about the case, giving your reader the prediction you are making. This is followed by the overall rule. The overall rule can come from a statute, case law, or both. The overall rule may be a synthesized rule that you have distilled from a number of cases. Next, you include policy *if* it is relevant to your prediction. Finally, the roadmap paragraph should alert the reader if there are issues that you are not going to address.

EXAMPLE: A roadmap paragraph where the overall rule comes from case law and includes policy.

Here the issue is the enforceability of a non-compete clause in a client's contract in Nebraska. A non-compete clause is a common part of an employment contract that restricts an employee from leaving employment and immediately using assets like goodwill, training, trade secrets, or client lists to compete against the employer.

DISCUSSION

The non-compete clause in Lyle Lovell's contract is likely not enforceable because it covered more geographic territory than reasonably necessary to protect Sunshine's legitimate business interest in its driver education company. Typically, a non-compete clause is only enforceable when it is (1) not greater than is reasonably necessary to protect the employer in some legitimate interest, (2) not unduly harsh and oppressive on the employee, and (3) reasonable in the sense that it is not injurious to the public. *Mertz v. Pharmacists Mut. Ins. Co.*, 625 N.W.2d 197, 204 (Neb. 2001). Failure to meet any of the three elements is grounds to invalidate the provision and reformation of unreasonable provisions is not allowed. *Vlasin v. Len Johnson & Co., Inc.*, 455 N.W.2d 772, 776 (Neb. 1990). This test promotes a reasonable balance between the employer's interests, the employee's prospects, and the public good. See *Dow v. Gotch*, 201 N.W. 655, 657 (Neb. 1924); *Am. Sec. Ser., Inc. v. Vodra*, 385 N.W.2d 73, 80 (Neb. 1986).

Overall conclusion

Overall rule based on common law

Policy

EXAMPLE: A roadmap paragraph where the overall rule is based on case law and policy is not included.

This excerpt is from the sample memorandum on page 9.

DISCUSSION

Albert's prior act involving the turkey is relevant for a purpose other than character because she raised the issue of intent, and the prior act is factually similar and close in time to the charged act. Evidence is relevant for a purpose other than character if it (1) has a direct bearing on an issue actually in dispute, and (2) a clear and logical connection exists between that act and the crime charged. *McGlew*, 658 A.2d at 1194. The trial court must make specific findings on each of these elements. *Id.*

Overall conclusion

Overall rule from case law

EXAMPLE: A roadmap paragraph where the overall rule is based on a statute and case law.

Here the issue is whether the client, who was having car trouble, "trespassed" when she entered a home after knocking. The homeowner had not heard the knocking and was surprised by the client inside the house.

Overall conclusion

Statutory rule

Further statement of overall rule based on case law

> There is insufficient evidence against our client, Ms. Carter, that she knew she was neither licensed nor privileged to enter Mr. Hall's residence, and thus a conviction against her for trespass is unlikely. Vermont's criminal trespass statute, based on the Model Penal Code, forbids an actor from enter[ing] a dwelling house, whether or not a person is actually present, knowing that [s]he is not licensed or privileged to do so. 13 V.S.A. § 3705(d) (2006). (*See also* Model Penal Code §221.2(1) (1962)). The knowledge requirement establishes a subjective standard. It is not sufficient for the state to show that the defendant should have known the entrant was not licensed or privileged to enter the dwelling. *State v. Fanger,* 164 Vt. 48, 52, 665 A.2d 36, 38 (Vt. 1995).

CASE FILE 1: Assignment—Roadmap Paragraph

Write out the roadmap paragraph for the discussion section of the Potter memorandum.

2. Explaining the Law Using Case Examples

Once you have done an outline and constructed your roadmap paragraph, where you give the overall rule that will answer the client's problem, you will, in the following paragraphs, break down the rule and show the reader how you arrived at your conclusions about the client's case. Each paragraph explaining the law should begin with a principle or focused point that you will explain in the paragraph. Paragraphs in legal writing are like division problems. The answer to the particular problem is on top of the equation. The contents of the paragraph are where you "show your work" to justify for the reader that your conclusion is right.

How you "show your work" will depend on the type of problem. Typically, the explanation of the law entails using cases to show by example how the court has applied each relevant piece of the rule to different factual settings that resemble the facts of your case. Case examples will be helpful in both analogizing your client's facts and distinguishing your client's facts. Remember, our system of law depends on *stare decisis.* Correctly predicting or advocating for a particular result will depend on what courts have done in the past, thus, comparing past cases to your case is key to an accurate and thorough analysis of the law.

Each paragraph should start with the conclusion being supported or explained. Sometimes it will take more than one paragraph to explain a conclusion. In this case, use a clear transition at the start of the paragraph to alert the reader that you are continuing to support the same conclusion.

Using words like "similarly," "likewise," or "on the other hand" will tell the reader that you are still explaining the same conclusion as in the preceding paragraph.

3. A Step-by-Step Approach to Writing the Explanation of the Law

Step 1: Start with a principle or focused point that is a sentence or two. State the point or the legal principle that the case explanation will clarify and prove to be true. These sentences are referred to as "hooks" or "conclusion" sentences. This sentence should be specific and should explicitly connect the reader to the part of the overall rule in the roadmap paragraph that you are addressing. You will learn more specifically how to write these sentences in Chapter 9. Use the present tense when stating the focus sentence or legal principle. Notice in the example below that the first conclusion sentence uses the same term "legitimate business interest" to alert the reader that this is the term that will be defined in the paragraph. The first sentence of the next paragraph further breaks down the meaning of "legitimate business interest" and draws the reader's attention to the definition of "unfair competition."

DISCUSSION

The non-compete clause in Lyle Lovell's contract is likely not enforceable because it covered more geographic territory than reasonably necessary to protect Sunshine's legitimate business interest in its driver education company. Typically, a non-compete clause is only enforceable when it is (1) not greater than is reasonably necessary to protect the employer in some legitimate interest, (2) not unduly harsh and oppressive on the employee, and (3) reasonable in the sense that it is not injurious to the public. *Mertz v. Pharmacists Mut. Ins. Co.,* 625 N.W.2d 197, 204 (Neb. 2001). Failure to meet any of the three elements is grounds to invalidate the provision and reformation of unreasonable provisions is not allowed. *Vlasin v. Len Johnson & Co., Inc.,* 455 N.W.2d 772, 776 (Neb. 1990). This test promotes a reasonable balance between the employer's interests, the employee's prospects, and the public good. *See Dow v. Gotch,* 201 N.W. 655, 657 (Neb. 1924); *Am. Sec. Ser., Inc. v. Vodra,* 385 N.W.2d 73, 80 (Neb. 1986).

Overall conclusion

Overall rule based on common law

Policy

An employer has a legitimate business interest in protection against improper and unfair competition, but not against use of general skills or knowledge obtainable from a similar business. *Moore,* 562 N.W.2d at 540; *Boisen,* 383 N.W.2d at 34. *Polly v. Ray D. Hilderman & Co.,* 407 N.W.2d 751, 755 (Neb. 1987) Unfair competition is distinguished from ordinary competition by evaluating an employee's opportunity to appropriate goodwill from the employer. *Boisen,* 383 N.W.2d at 33. For example, in *Polly,* where an accountant had substantial personal contact with approximately 46 of his employer's accounts, the court found that the accounting firm had a legitimate interest in protecting itself against the accountant's opportunity to appropriate customer goodwill after his employment was terminated. *Polly,* 407 N.W. 2d at 756.

Conclusion sentence that focuses on one part of the overall rule—definition of legitimate business interest. Next, writer defines unfair competition. Finally, writer shows an example of how a court has applied the term "unfair competition."

Step 2: Construct your case description.

Before you write about the cases that serve as examples of how the court applies the legal principles you base your prediction on, you need to have done the necessary background thinking. To write an effective case description, you need to have first studied and distilled what the key cases hold. This means you must:

- Identify the court's holding (or the court's answer to the relevant legal question before it).
- Identify the court's reasoning (why the court decided the relevant legal question the way it did).
- Identify critical/legally significant facts in the case.
- Identify the legal principle that the case illustrates (the "focus sentence").

Step 3: Write the case description.

Include only critical/legally significant facts and any context facts necessary for the reader to understand the case: reasoning and holding.

Step 4: Do's and don'ts.

- DO use the past tense when describing a case.
- DON'T use party names, instead use party designations. For example, instead of using Mr. Winstead (from case file 1: Winstead case), use "defendant." Other designations can include "plaintiff" or descriptors such as "patron," "driver," or "employer." Designating the parties by the roles they play in the case will make it easier for your reader to understand the legal principles addressed in the case.

EXAMPLE:

NOT HELPFUL: Here, the writer uses names, making it difficult to discern the significance of the parties' roles.

For example, in *Polly*, where Mr. Polly had substantial personal contact with approximately 46 of Hilderman's accounts, the court found that Hilderman had a legitimate interest in protecting itself against Polly's opportunity to appropriate customer goodwill after his employment was terminated. *Polly, 407 N.W. 2d at 756.*

HELPFUL: Here, the writer uses designations. Notice that significance of the parties' actions are easier to discern.

For example, in *Polly*, where an accountant had substantial personal contact with approximately 46 of his employer's accounts, the court found that the accounting firm had a legitimate interest in protecting itself against the accountant's opportunity to appropriate customer goodwill after his employment was terminated. *Polly, 407 N.W. 2d at 756.*

- Give the reader only necessary information. Don't include procedural information unless it is critical to the issue. Don't include background facts other than to give the description necessary context.

EXAMPLE:

NOT HELPFUL: The procedural information here is not decisively relevant to the key issue—the enforceability of the non-compete clause.

For example, in *Polly*, the plaintiff appealed a wage collection decision of the district court sustaining the plaintiff's motion for summary judgment and the court affirmed the district court's decision. *Polly, 407 N.W. 2d at 753.* The court found that the accounting firm had a legitimate interest in protecting itself against the accountant's opportunity to appropriate customer goodwill after his employment was terminated. *Id at 756.* The ruling was based on the accountant having had substantial personal contact with approximately 46 of his employer's accounts. *Id.*

In *Holloran*, on March 15, 1994, police found the inebriated defendant asleep in Londonderry, New Hampshire, in the driver's seat of his pickup truck with the keys in the ignition; he was awaiting a phone call from his wife to pick her up from a Tupperware party. *Id.* at 800.

> NOT HELPFUL: Reader does not need to know the date or the exact place where the incident occurred.

- When using more than one case to illustrate the legal principle, be sure to connect the cases, making it clear to the reader why the cases are being addressed within the same paragraph (or paragraphs) to prove a principle. Using words like "similarly," "likewise," or "in contrast" will alert your reader about how the cases should be read together.
- Avoid writing a report of cases. Remember that the reader needs more than just what each case said. The reader needs to understand the principle and the cases help exemplify those principles. If each paragraph begins with "In [case name]" the reader has no context for why the case is relevant.

Evidence of a prior act is relevant to refute a defendant's claim that the crime was committed by accident. *Lesnick*, 677 A.2d at 690. For example, the court in *Lesnick* admitted evidence of a prior act because it was relevant to show the absence of an accident where the defendant claimed she had stabbed her husband in self-defense because she believed him to be an unknown intruder. *Id.* In contrast, where the defendant denied any involvement at all in the crime, the court excluded the evidence. *State v. Blackey*, 623 A.2d 1331, 1332-33 (N.H. 1993). The evidence was not relevant because, by denying the crime altogether, the defendant had not placed her intent at issue. *Id.*

> HELPFUL: Sentence that identifies the legal principle described in the paragraph below.
>
> Court's holding
>
> Court's reasoning

CASE FILE 1: Assignment—Write a Case Example

Write a paragraph that uses *Winstead* to illustrate a legal principle.

- Start with the legal principle that the case description will clarify or prove.
- Include the relevant, legally significant facts.
- Include the court's holding on the legal principle.
- Include the court's reasoning.
- If you think more than one case supports the principle, complete the paragraph using additional cases.

D. APPLYING THE LAW IN A DISCUSSION

Because our legal system is grounded in *stare decisis,* legal analysis is typically supported by precedent cases. Ultimately, whomever you are writing an analysis for will want assurance that there is ample support for the prediction you are making. The reader will want to see that you are a reliable legal analyst. Judges have a particular reason for wanting to get the law right—they want to exercise their judgment fairly. Although your first internships and summer jobs may not require you to write a persuasive analysis for a judge, your supervisors may use the work you do to persuade a judge of a particular position on behalf of a client. Your analysis may also be needed to demonstrate to a client that a particular position is supported. Here, too, you will need ample precedent to justify your position.

Explaining the law, using specific examples of how courts have applied legal principles to problems similar to the client's, is the first step in an effective legal analysis. The next step is showing the reader *why* the prior cases support your prediction. Writing case comparisons requires explicitness and precision. There is no use to the reader in broad legal conclusions without specific support. This section will provide you with an approach to writing a case comparison.

Effective case comparisons require that you know your client's facts. You will need to comb through the client facts and identify those that matter to an outcome. Similar to the decisive facts cited by the court in an opinion, your client's decisive facts are the ones that decide the issue. Refer to discussion about background versus decisive facts on page 60. Take away a particular fact, and the outcome changes. You won't be able to judge the relevant client facts until you know the law. Once you understand the law, you can figure out which facts matter by comparing client facts to the critical facts from cases.

The application of the law to your client's problem builds upon the explanation of the relevant law. The explanation of the law and the application should form a parallel structure. The case examples you use to show how a court has applied the rule in other situations should match up with the facts you are focusing on in your client's case. Thus, once you have the explanation of the law done, you can begin to construct your comparisons—both the analogies and the distinctions. Keep in mind the legal rule that will be applied, the court's reasoning, and the outcome you are predicting as you proceed through the following steps.

1. Identify critical/legally significant facts in the prior case (i.e., the one you're using to make the analogy). Remember, these are the facts that the court's holding turns on.

2. Identify critical/legally significant facts in your client's case.

3. Identify how the critical facts make your case similar to or different from the prior case. Important note: If you can't make a direct, one-to-one fact comparison, you may still be able to make the analogy or distinction by focusing on a different level of comparison; for example, you can't compare apples to oranges, but at a more abstract level, both are fruit. The case facts may also be so different that they help prove your point. For

example, let's say in Dr. Potter's case there was an opinion, we will call it Case A, where the defendant had gone off the road, turned off the car, and moved to the back seat. Let's say further that the court justified finding that the defendant was not "driving" by reasoning that these facts all proved that he had no intent to drive and that they showed no indicia of control over the car. The case could be useful in deciding if Dr. Potter was "driving." Even though the facts are different, you can contrast, or distinguish, Dr. Potter's facts that he was in the driver's seat compared to the driver in Case A, who was in the back seat. Since the court found that being in the back seat demonstrated no intent to drive, Case A might reach the opposite conclusion (intent to drive) in Dr. Potter's situation.

4. Identify the legal significance of the overlapping facts. In other words, use the reasoning that the court applied in the prior decision to predict what the outcome will be when the rule is applied in your client's case.

5. Construct your comparison or distinction:
   Start with a sentence in which you state the point the analogy is intended to make.

   EXAMPLE A: Sentence that *does not state* the point of the analogy

   "Albert's case is similar to the facts of *Lesnick*." This sentence does not tell the reader the substance of why the case comparison matters.

   EXAMPLE B: Sentence *that states* the point of the analogy

   "Albert's prior act is relevant here because Albert claims she took the ham by accident." This sentence tells the reader why the comparison matters.

6. Write the rest of the analogy:
   Compare the critical facts in your client's case and the critical facts in the prior case. Make sure to use the appropriate level of detail. Be specific and concrete, but don't include any nonessential facts.

   EXAMPLE A: Analogy that lacks sufficient, decisive detail:

   "Like the defendant in *Lesnick*, where the prior act was admitted, here Albert's prior act should be similarly admitted." Notice that the writer is comparing broad legal concepts instead of specific significant facts.

   EXAMPLE B: Analogy with sufficient, decisive detail:

   "Like the defendant in *Lesnick*, who admitted the stabbing but claimed it was an accident, Albert made her intent an issue by claiming she took the ham unintentionally." Notice the explicit detail.

   Analogies that lack sufficient depth and detail fail to provide the reader with a reliable justification for your conclusion on the problem.
   Here are some ways to help the reader understand the comparison:
   a. Place the facts from the two cases close together.
   b. Explicitly make the comparison using words like "like" or "similar to" or "unlike."

      c. Use parallel structure.

      d. Compare like items.

7. Use "because"! So much of legal analysis requires you to justify why you think a particular outcome is likely. Explain why the comparison matters by applying the reasoning from the prior case to your client's facts. In this way, you inform the reader of the legal significance of the similarity/difference between your client's facts and the facts in the prior case. For example: "Therefore, *because* evidence of the prior act is offered for a purpose other than Albert's character or propensity to steal meat, it is probably admissible."

EXAMPLE: Giving the specific reasoning that supports your prediction.

> Covenants that are unduly broad in scope as to time, geography, or activity are void as a matter of public policy, because they hinder competition and free trade. *See Mertz v. Pharmacists Mut. Ins. Co.,* 625 N.W.2d 197, 204 (Neb. 2001). For example, in *Mertz,* a three-year territorial covenant was unenforceable <u>because the covenant summarily precluded all solicitation within the territory rather than being reasonably limited to those customers that he had worked with directly.</u> *Id.* at 204.

> The courts are likely to view Reno's non-compete restriction as overly broad and unenforceable. Like the three-year non-compete clause in *Mertz,* that was invalidated because it encompassed customers with whom the employee had never had any contact, Reno's non-compete agreement similarly includes a blanket prohibition that precludes him from soliciting new customers or new markets. <u>The court is likely to invalidate such a clause, as it did in *Mertz*, because it is not narrowly tailored to cover only those customers who Reno had previously contacted.</u>

The underlined portions show the reasoning that supports the prediction.

8. Writing an effective analogy or distinction should help you discover if you have not adequately given decisive facts from a case. The case examples and the analogies and distinctions should focus on the same facts. In other words, the case comparisons in the application of the law should use the facts described in the case explanations. The two sections should include parallel analysis.

EXAMPLE: Explanation of law and application of law—parallel structure with similar use of decisive facts.

The highlighted portions indicate the parallel structure. Notice that each excerpt zeroes in on specific facts.

> Covenants that are unduly broad in scope as to time, geography, or activity are void as a matter of public policy, because they hinder competition and free trade. *See Mertz v. Pharmacists Mut. Ins. Co.,* 625 N.W.2d 197, 204 (Neb. 2001). For example, in *Mertz,* a three-year territorial covenant was unenforceable because the covenant summarily precluded all solicitation

within the territory rather than being reasonably limited to those customers that he had worked with directly. *Id.* at 204.

The courts are likely to view Reno's non-compete restriction as overly broad and unenforceable. Like the three-year non-compete clause in *Mertz*, that was invalidated because it encompassed customers with whom the employee had never had any contact, Reno's non-compete agreement similarly includes a blanket prohibition that precludes him from soliciting new customers or new markets. The court is likely to invalidate such a clause, as it did in *Mertz*, because it is not narrowly tailored to cover only those customers whom Reno had previously contacted.

CASE FILE 1: Assignment—Write a Case Comparison

Write one case comparison that either analogizes or distinguishes Potter facts to one of the cases in case file 1.

E. ORGANIZATION: INTERNAL PARAGRAPH STRUCTURE

At this point, you have a draft of part of the analysis for case file 1. You have studied the law, completed an outline, and written a case illustration and a case comparison. As you move into drafting the complete analysis, pay attention to how the structure hangs together. You want your reader to move easily through the analysis, going from paragraph to paragraph without being interrupted by a point or sentence that does not seem to flow from the roadmap you have provided in the first paragraphs of the discussion section.

Legal analysis must be tightly constructed. The structure begins with the overall paragraph or roadmap. The paragraphs that follow should flesh out the legal principles identified in the roadmap paragraph. Each of these paragraphs must be constructed carefully using language that alerts your reader to the point you are supporting. At its most basic level, your writing will have an emotional impact on your reader. A reaction of ease and confidence is what you are hoping for, not frustration and confusion.

To ensure good structure, first draft the outline (see section B above). This will serve as a guide to keep your overall structure on target. The outline should instruct you about the order in which your points must proceed. Once you begin to draft your analysis, follow these rules when writing your paragraphs:

1. Only address one point per paragraph.
2. Keep the paragraphs that explain the law and give examples from the cases separate from paragraphs that apply the law to your client's fact.

3. Begin each paragraph with a clear conclusion that tells the reader the point of the paragraph or with an obvious transition word that signals to the reader that the paragraph is substantively connected to the one preceding.

4. Keep the paragraphs short—no more than one-half a page, but preferably less.

1. Writing the Paragraph's First Sentence

The point of every paragraph should appear in the first sentence. This sentence should be clear and decisive. For example, when you read the following paragraph, do you know immediately the point of the paragraph? What is the writer's conclusion regarding the substance within this paragraph?

EXAMPLE A:

> In *Milano,* the court held the evidence allowed a reasonable inference that the bar served the intoxicated driver alcohol despite the server's claim that she refused to sell him alcohol. *Milano,* 506 A.2d at 163, 164-165. The court reasoned the jury could have believed the driver entered the bar sober and left intoxicated where the driver got into an accident two blocks from the bar and was intoxicated at the scene of the accident. *Id.*at 165.

Now, read the following paragraph. Can you easily know the paragraph's point?

EXAMPLE B:

> Even without direct evidence of a bar's sale to a patron, a jury could find that a sale occurred from circumstantial evidence. For example, in *Milano,* the jury permissibly drew an inference that the bar sold to the intoxicated driver where the driver entered the bar sober and left intoxicated and got into an accident two blocks from the bar. *Id.* at 165. In addition, the driver was intoxicated at the scene of the accident, providing further circumstantial evidence from which the jury could infer that the bar sold alcohol to the driver. *Id.*at 165.

In example B, the writer has decisively alerted the reader to the point of the paragraph. The sentence comfortably orients the reader. By contrast, in example A the writer begins with a case and the reader has no idea *why* that case is being discussed. The busy reader will react more favorably when the writer carefully walks him or her through the paragraph.

Here is how you might go about developing a paragraph's decisive and clear first sentence:

1. The idea emerges in draft form.

> The New Hampshire courts look at the nature of the prior act when deciding on its admission. Cite.

What does this tell the reader about how the rule works? (identifies nature of prior act as important)

But what is it about the nature of the prior act that is important for the reader to understand?

2. The writer refines the point of the paragraph.

> To determine the admissibility of a prior bad act, the New Hampshire courts analyze the relevance to the current charge. Cite.

What does this tell the reader about how the rule works? (how relevant it is)

What is missing? (connection to the overall rule's purpose)

3. The writer specifically identifies the purpose of the rule and the point of the paragraph with the opening sentence.

> Courts determine whether a prior bad act is admissible by examining whether the prior act evidence is relevant because it specifically refutes the defendant's current defense. Cite. For example…

What does this tell the reader about how the rule works? (relevance linked to refutation of defendant's defense)

4. The writer refines and sharpens the language, making the point precise and clear.

> Evidence of a prior act is relevant to refute defendant's claim that the crime was committed by accident. Cite. For example in…

2. Using Parallel Structure

Your analysis will be organized into paragraphs that explain the law followed by paragraphs that apply the law. Even though these paragraphs are doing different things, use the same structure in each. This will also help your reader to easily move through your analysis. In the paragraphs below, notice the parallel structure.

EXAMPLE: Explanation of law paragraph

> Evidence of a prior act is relevant to refute a defendant's claim that the crime was committed by accident. *Lesnick*, 677 A.2d at 690. For example, the court in Lesnick admitted evidence of a prior act because it was relevant to show the absence of an accident where the defendant claimed she had stabbed her husband in self-defense because she believed him to be an unknown intruder. Id. In contrast, where the defendant denied any involvement at all in the crime, the court excluded the evidence. *State v. Blackey*, 623 A.2d 1333, 1334 (N.H. 1993). It reasoned that the evidence was not relevant because, by denying the crime altogether, the defendant had not placed her intent or propensity at issue. *Id.* at 1334; *State v. Whittaker*, 642 A.2d 936, 938 (N.H. 1994).

The conclusion sentence: tells the reader the legal principle you are explaining.

Case information with illustrations.

The reasoning or rationale the court gives to justify its conclusion.

EXAMPLE: Application of law paragraph

The conclusion sentence: tells the reader the legal principle you are applying to your client's facts.

Case information where illustrations are applied to client facts.

The reasoning or rationale the writer gives to justify legal conclusion.

Albert's prior act is likely relevant here because she claims she took the ham by accident. Like the defendant in Lesnick, who admitted the stabbing but claimed it was an accident, Albert made her intent an issue by claiming she took the ham unintentionally. Evidence of a prior similar act is relevant to disproving Albert's claim of accident because the two similar acts close in time indicate her intent to shoplift. Therefore, because the evidence of the prior act is offered for a purpose other than Albert's character or propensity to steal meat, it probably is admissible.

CHAPTER 8

Client Letters

A. CLIENT LETTERS

Client letters can cover many topics, but there are two common types: a retainment letter and a letter summarizing the probable outcome of your client's case. The example on page 20 is the second type, where the lawyer explains the probable outcome of a client's case.

1. Organization

A client letter that gives a client a prediction in his or her case follows the basic IRAC structure that you are now used to. Below is an example with labels in the margin to identify the IRAC (or CREAC) structure.

Carl Client
3 West Street
Town, State

Re: Liz Baker's Law Degree as Marital Property

As requested, this letter will give you my opinion about whether your former wife's law degree and its attendant monetary value are marital property under our state's law. Since our last meeting, I have studied the relevant law in relation to your facts. Since you and Liz jointly decided that she should attend law school, it is likely that the degree and its value is marital property. The valuation of the degree will have to be assessed by an expert and therefore this letter will not address that issue.

Explanation of Relevant Law

Marital property means all property acquired by spouses during the marriage. Earned degrees generally constitute marital property where the couple jointly decided how to develop their future earning capacity to support their family by sending one party to school. Our courts view marriage as a partnership and, when a marriage ends, each of the spouses, based on the totality of the contributions made to it, has a stake in and right to a share of the marital property. This is because that property represents the capital product of the partnership.

In cases of long-term marriages where the parties jointly decided how to raise their family, manage their future earning capacity, and had shared expectations of future material benefit, the court usually awards a sum representing the fair distribution of the professional degree. The court will also consider the sacrifices made by a spouse who did not earn the professional degree. When a supporting spouse sacrifices a career or makes a significant financial contribution toward the spouse's professional education with the expectation that both parties would enjoy material benefits flowing from the degree, the court will likely view the degree as marital property.

The Likely Outcome of This Issue

You will likely be awarded a sum representing a fair distribution of Liz's law degree. You and Liz have a long-term marriage and you decided together that she would get her degree first while you managed the home and the children. In addition, you sacrificed by putting off attending graduate school. Because you and Liz jointly agreed on this course of action for the benefit of the family, the court will likely award you a fair distribution of the degree. Liz's attorney will likely argue that the future monetary value is uncertain and unquantifiable. However, the court has rejected this argument in cases similar to yours. Moreover, if we have a credible expert to calculate the degree's value, the court is likely to accept our position.

Conclusion and Next Steps

Based on my preliminary research, it appears that Liz's law degree will be a marital asset. Our next step is to discuss hiring an expert to value the degree. These experts can be expensive, so we should discuss whether you would like to pursue this course. I suggest sending Liz's lawyer a letter outlining our position on her law degree. Perhaps we can resolve this aspect of your divorce through negotiation and agreement. Let me know if you have any questions or concerns.

Sincerely,
Lawyer

2. Content

Your reader may be another lawyer, a sophisticated government official, a businessperson, or a layperson. Frequently, several people with varying backgrounds may read your letter; for example, a board of directors or a group of small business owners or planning board members. Write so that your reader(s) can understand you. Keep in mind that client letters also serve as a helpful summary of the case. If you are working on a complex case that stretches over a long period of time, the client letters can serve as helpful tools to remember what has happened in the case.

Tailor your tone to your relationship with the client. Be respectful, specific, and candid. Keep in mind that you are a professional; do not use slang or "text speak," but be direct.

Write in plain English, avoid legalese, and keep sentences short and concise. Use short paragraphs. Your reader should be able to understand your writing without asking for a translator. Avoid all ambiguities.

3. Retainment Letters

When a client hires a lawyer, typically the terms of the engagement are set forth in a retainment letter. The letter, very much like a contract, usually sets out what services the lawyer will perform and at what cost. Law firms and individual lawyers often have standard retention letters that are personalized for individual cases.

B. E-MAIL CORRESPONDENCE FORMAT

Lawyers communicate primarily by e-mail, whether it is with a client, another lawyer, or other professional. You will likely communicate with prospective employers via e-mail as early as the winter of your first year in law school. In law school, you will e-mail your professors, the law school staff, and fellow students. Here are a few rules of the road to follow:

1. *E-mail with your professors and the law school staff.* Treat all communication with law school personnel (faculty and staff) as professional correspondence. This is a good time to practice good habits. Here are some guidelines:
   - Identify the content of the e-mail with a proper subject line. Do not find an old e-mail with an unrelated subject and reply to it without changing the subject line. Format the subject line properly. Use capital letters and a brief (one to four words) description of the e-mail's nature.
   - Use a proper salutation, as in "Dear Professor Carter" or "Dear Ms. Jones" (if it is a staff member).

- Use proper English in the body of the e-mail. Do not use abbreviations, slang, or text speak. Do not be overly formal or use legal jargon.
- Proofread carefully. It will matter to your recipient and reflect poorly on your abilities if he or she receives an e-mail that has typos or misspellings.
- Be respectful and deferential in your tone.

2. ***E-mail with clients or other lawyers.*** You will likely begin to e-mail with other lawyers during your first year of law school. Once you are in a summer placement, you may be asked to draft an e-mail to a client or another lawyer. Apply the rules above to these types of e-mails. Follow the guidelines on client letters above and apply them to e-mail correspondence. They will be structured the same except that the address and contact information should be part of the signature. In addition, you will want to include a confidentiality statement as part of the signature block. Check with your employer about the proper contents of your signature block. If the content is longer than an e-mail screen, put the letter in PDF form and attach it to the e-mail.

A typical e-mail signature looks like this:

Susan Barkley

abarkey@workemail.com
623-233-1234 direct
623-233-2333 main
Barkley Law Offices
7 Hathaway St
Anytown, NY 23456

Confidentiality notice: This message is intended only for the person to whom addressed in the text above and may contain privileged or confidential information. If you are not that person, any use of this message is prohibited. We request that you notify us by reply to this message, and then delete all copies of this message including any contained in your reply. Thank you.

C. E-MAIL CORRESPONDENCE SUBSTANCE

Many times an e-mail to another lawyer or to a client will be for the same purpose as a legal memorandum—to offer an objective analysis of the law that predicts a likely outcome in a case. Thus, the memorandum will either be attached to an e-mail or contained in the body of the e-mail.

Either way, the memorandum content that you will learn should apply or be easily adapted to the e-mail format.

D. A FINAL CAUTIONARY MESSAGE

Most employers have an e-mail and Internet policy, and you should ask to see it once you begin your employment. Employers have the right to read your work e-mails and monitor your Internet usage, and most do. Moreover, your e-mails may become the subject of a request that a litigant asks for as part of a discovery process. Thus, when you draft an e-mail, consider that your audience may end up being wider than the recipient. Your reputation, credibility, and ability are all at stake with just about every legal correspondence you author. Use the *New York Times* rule on e-mailing (also known as the "Front Page of the Newspaper" Test): "Don't do anything you wouldn't want published on the front page of the *New York Times*."

CHAPTER 9

Revising

You may remember from the introduction that revising makes up a large percentage of the writing process. The different kinds of revising—large-scale, internal paragraph, and micro (grammar and mechanics)—will be discussed in this chapter.

A. LARGE-SCALE REVISING

One way to check if your analysis has a solid organization is to deconstruct it. Here is a strategy for assessing your organization.

Highlight each paragraph's first sentence, or cut and paste each first sentence into a separate document. Each sentence, standing alone, should logically show the lay out of your argument. If one of the sentences lacks a clear focus, it will interrupt the logical flow of your stand-alone sentences.

Look at the sentences below. They are the first sentence from each paragraph in the sample on page 9. Notice how they represent an organized logic.

> Albert's prior act involving the turkey is relevant for a purpose other than character because she raised the issue of intent, and the prior act is factually similar and close in time to the charged act.

> ***Direct Bearing on Issue in Dispute***
> Evidence of a prior act is relevant to refute a defendant's claim that the crime was committed by accident. *Lesnick*, 677 A.2d at 690.

> Albert's prior act is likely relevant here because she claims she took the ham by accident.

> ***Clear and Logical Connection***
> Next, the evidence probably meets the second prong of the relevancy analysis because a clear, logical connection exists between the charged act of stealing a ham and the prior act of taking a turkey.

Where two acts are significantly different, the court will not admit evidence of the first one to prove the defendant's intent in committing the second act.

In Albert's case, the turkey and the ham were similar products removed from the same store, using the same method of removal—all facts that show that the second incident was not an accident.

Moreover, the close time frame between Albert's two incidents further strengthens their connection.

B. INTERNAL PARAGRAPH REVISING: REVERSE OUTLINE

This strategy will help you to practice critically reading and evaluating what you have written so that you can make your document more effective. Reverse outlining gives you the real picture of your argument **as it is currently written**. By going through the task of naming what you have done and seeing the document in its true skeletal form, you can get a better perspective on what is on the page and how you can start to make it more effective. *This is a technique you can use for any writing to ensure that what you have written is what you meant to say, and to see how the parts of the writing work together.*

1. First, read the entire section (sub-issue) without stopping.
2. Re-read and note what is **actually present** in the writing (not what you think *should* be there or what you plan to have there or what was in your initial outline, unless that is exactly what is there). Describe what you see. In particular, note if you see explanation of law or application of client facts to law.
3. Note the overall point of each paragraph.
4. Note the point of each sentence in the paragraph.
5. Read the reverse outline, looking for:
   - *Organization.* Does the structure of the discussion section work logically? Is it set out in a way that the reader can follow?
   - *Content.* Do the authorities being used "flesh out" the analysis? Do the authorities used fully show the analysis?
   - *Depth of analysis.* Are cases summarized/synthesized before being described individually? Are the authorities analyzed around principles? Are decisive facts, holding, and reasoning noted where appropriate? Are facts analogized and distinguished?
   - *Gaps and ambiguities.* Having reverse outlined the section, what gaps do you notice? Do the paragraphs include transitions and show how they relate? Does each paragraph have one main point? Do the parts of the analysis have introductory road maps? Are there inconsistencies? Are the assumptions appropriate?

C. MICRO REVISING: GRAMMAR AND MECHANICS

You may be surprised to find a section on grammar in a textbook for law students. You probably had grammar training at some point in your education, but it may have been a while ago. Consider this a refresher. Take grammar seriously. Law students juggle many new concepts as they master legal writing, which can lead to cognitive overload. The tips provided here are meant to make proofreading a bit easier, but there is no substitute for careful proofreading. A common lament of practicing lawyers is that new lawyers seem to ignore basic rules of grammar, so paying attention to the details is well worth the time.

It is important to master a few basic grammar and stylistic points. Beyond that, keep a grammar and style book handy throughout law school and after.

1. Generally, avoid passive voice.
    *   A "be" verb plus a past participle (a verb ending in –ed) can indicate passive voice.
        Example: Is dismissed; are docketed; was vacated = passive voice.
    *   To rewrite sentences in the active voice, ask yourself, "Who is doing what to whom in this sentence?" then rewrite the sentence to focus on the actor, the action, and the object (if there is an object).
    *   The word "by" can indicate passive voice.
        Example: The sentence was commuted by the governor vs. The governor commuted the sentence.

        EXAMPLE: Sentence with passive voice

        The four factors <u>to be</u> taken into account in <u>considering</u> a request for the entry of a preliminary injunction are…

        EXAMPLE: Same sentence edited

        A court considers four factors in deciding whether to impose a preliminary injunction. The factors are….

2. Omit surplus words
    *   Replace four or five words with one or two.

        EXAMPLE: Too many words

        The fact that the court repeatedly ruled against the defendant was evidence of its bias.

        Example: Omitting the excess

        The court's repeated denials of the defendant's objections indicated its bias.

3. Use base verbs, not nominalizations
   - Legal readers want you to be clear and concrete. Use verbs to describe the action.
     Examples: act vs. action; conclude vs. making conclusions.
   - A nominalization is a verb turned into a noun. You can spot a nominalization by its ending. Endings associated with nominalizations include:

-al	-ment	-ant	-ence
-ion	-ent	-ancy	-ency
-ance	-ity		

     Example: The defendant's request is that his sentence be reduced vs. *The defendant requests a sentence reduction.*
   - Not all words with these endings are nominalizations, and not all nominalizations are "bad." If you see a word with one of these endings, however, stop to see if you can make your sentence shorter or stronger by using a base verb instead.

4. Avoid words that lead to vague or imprecise sentences
   - There are some "buzz" words to avoid. Words like "involve," "whether," or "the court considers" inevitably lead to a sentence that does not take a position.
     Example: Decisions on preliminary injunctions involve several factors. vs. *A court considers four factors in deciding whether to impose a preliminary injunction.*

     ### EXAMPLE: Wordy

     In determining whether a suspect comprehends the consequence of the Fifth Amendment waiver, the Supreme Court does not require that every consequence <u>is known by</u> the defendant, only that the waiver <u>is made</u> voluntarily, knowingly, and intelligently.

     ### EXAMPLE: Better

     The Supreme Court does not require that a suspect comprehend every possible consequence of the Fifth Amendment waiver, only that the waiver is voluntary, knowing, and intelligent.

     ### EXAMPLE: Wordy/Imprecise

     When the defendant is a native whose language is not English, identifying a legal waiver requires looking at whether the defendant conversed freely in English during questioning, and whether the law enforcement officers understood him.

     ### EXAMPLE: Better

     Proof that a non-English-speaking defendant has given a knowing and intelligent waiver includes evidence that the defendant conversed freely and understandably in English during questioning.

5. Use short sentences
   - If your sentences are long, check for passive voice, nominalizations, or vague language.
   - Do a random spot check and count words in a sentence. Average length should be below 25 words.
   - If necessary, chop up thoughts into two or more sentences.

6. Use transitions
   - Transitional phrases are used to show relationships between an individual paragraph and the preceding and succeeding ones.
   - They are helpful to the reader because they provide clarity, structure, and development of the paper.
   - "Moreover," "likewise," and "on the other hand" are examples of transitional words.

7. Use Microsoft Word to fix passive voice, grammar, and style
   - Find passive voice by doing a word find for "be," "been," etc.
   - The search shows you where the word "be" has led to a passive construction.
   - Be sure that your Word options are set to identify grammar and style problems (as well as spell check).

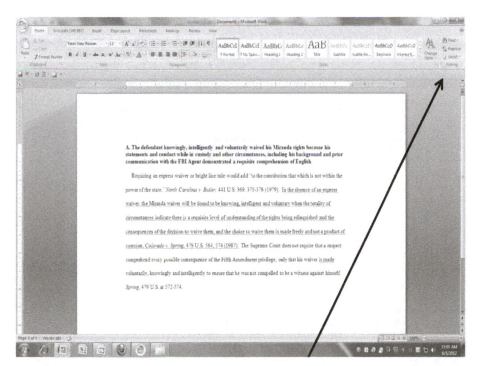

Where to look for "Find" in Word on a PC. On a Mac you can use "Search in Document."

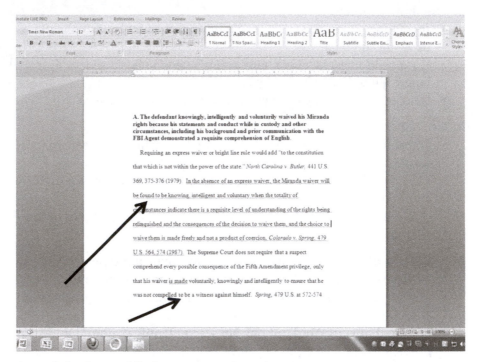

A search for the word "be" turns up passive voice.

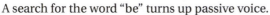

On a PC "Word Options" is how you set grammar checking. On a Mac, select "Spelling and Grammar" from the Tools menu.

On a PC, you set the type of Grammar and Style checking you want to use. On a Mac, once you have opened "Spelling and Grammar" select the "Options" button.

8. Remember that these are tools to help you spot writing issues; however, they are not substitutes for your own proofing and editing. This is especially true with spell check. Spell check will not always pick up a misspelled or incorrect word.
   Examples of spell check errors: The court reversed defendant's motion for a new trail; Defendant's councilor was present for the police line-up.

PART III

CASE FILE 2[1]
Lincoln Matthew, Jr.

---

1. This case file was adapted from a case file originally developed by Carrie Sperling at Sandra Day O'Connor School of Law. It is based on a real event that has been fictionalized for purposes of this textbook.

CHAPTER 10

Introduction to Case File 2

Case file 2 involves a client, Lincoln Matthew, Jr., who is a prominent professor at Harvard University in Cambridge, Massachusetts. Professor Matthew was arrested outside his home for disorderly conduct. Professor Matthew is considering filing a civil rights case against the Cambridge police. In order to file a civil law suit, Matthew would have to show that he was wrongly arrested. Case file 2 requires that you assess whether the behavior that led the police to arrest Matthew met the elements for disorderly conduct.

This case file will require you to write a whole legal memo including the issue, summary, facts, and discussion. The issue requires analysis of two sub-elements so you will have practice organizing a more complex legal discussion than you had for case file 1. Remember, learning how to write like a lawyer is a recursive process. You will build on many of the skills you learned in completing case file 1, including:

- Reading and understanding a statute
- Close case reading
- Briefing a case
- Deconstructing and synthesizing case law to form a rule
- Identifying key client facts
- Structuring an office memo using all the parts of a memo
- Formulating and writing an issue
- Writing an outline of the discussion section
- Organizing an analysis, including explaining the rule and applying the rule
- Writing the legal discussion of an objective interoffice memo

The new skills you will learn as you complete case file 2 include:

- Compiling facts from several documents
- Understanding hierarchy of authority in context
- Developing rules in a multi-issue case

- Writing an outline, draft, and final draft of a complete interoffice memo, including a fact section and legal discussion section
- Writing a roadmap paragraph that covers a multi-issue analysis
- Organizing two legal issues, including explaining the rule, applying the rule, and identifying how the two issues relate
- Identifying and addressing weaknesses or counterarguments

A. THE PROCESS FOR COMPLETING CASE FILE 2 MEMORANDUM

Remember that for case file 1 there was a step-by-step process for completing the project. Reprinted below, these are the same steps you will take as you tackle case file 2. Steps 2 and 3 have been done for you, so we will begin with step 1 and then move to step 4.

1. Understand the facts of your client's case.
2. Identify the area of law that is likely to hold the answer (e.g., employment law, medical malpractice law, criminal law)
3. Research law. This might start with reading a treatise or other secondary source.
4. Read and study relevant statutes and cases.
5. Identify the key fact from case law or legal principles that apply to your client's problem.
6. Review client's facts and identify the decisive facts.
7. Narrow the body of legal authority that addresses your client's problem—winnow out authority that is not on point.
8. Outline legal analysis.
9. Begin writing process.

MEMORANDUM

To: Associate
From: Supervising Attorney
Date: September XXX
Re: Lincoln Matthew, Jr.

Lincoln Matthew, Jr. has come to our firm seeking advice about his legal remedies. He was arrested and charged with disorderly conduct at his Cambridge home. The charges were later dropped. After meeting with Mr. Matthew, I am evaluating whether we could succeed in a civil rights action against the Cambridge Police Department officer who arrested Mr. Matthew for Mass. Gen. Law 272 sec. 53(b). I'm familiar with the federal civil rights laws. It is critical to our case to know whether Matthew actually engaged in disorderly conduct under the Massachusetts statute. If the police officer reasonably believed that Matthew committed disorderly conduct then we probably do not have a case under the civil rights law. I want you to review the relevant Massachusetts statute and case law and tell me whether **Matthew's conduct** constituted **disorderly conduct under the statute and case law**. I do not want you to analyze any aspect of the federal civil rights claim at this time.

As for the established law defining disorderly conduct in Massachusetts, another law clerk found the relevant statute and case law. Use these authorities to determine what the law was at the time of the arrest:

Mass. Gen. Laws Ann. Ch. 272 §53 (2008)
Commonwealth v. Sholley, 739 N.E.2d 236 (Mass. 2000).
Commonwealth v. Mulvey, 784 N.E.2d 1138 (Mass. App. 2003).
Commonwealth v. Lopiano, 805 N.E.2d 522 (Mass. App. 2004).
Levine v. Clement, 333 F. Supp. 2d 1 (D. Mass. 2004).

I have also provided you with all of the background facts that you need. They are contained in the sources I have listed below:

- The police reports
- Transcripts of the 911 tapes http://www.youtube.com/watch?v=ITI55WTyIRY

Please use only the information I have provided to you.

Cambridge Police
INCIDENT REPORT #2256

Date: July 17, 2014
Place: West St.
Incident Type/Offense: Disorderly Conduct c272 S53
Reporting Officer: Peter Smith

Offender: Lincoln Matthew, Jr.
Sex: Male
Race: Black
Age: 58

Narrative

On Thursday, July 17, 2014, Lincoln Matthew, Jr. (of West Street, Cambridge, MA) was placed under arrest at West Street, after being observed exhibiting loud and tumultuous behavior in a public place, directed at a uniformed police officer, who was present investigating a report of a crime in progress. These actions on the behalf of Matthew served no legitimate purpose and caused citizens passing by this location to stop and take notice while appearing surprised and alarmed.

On the above time and date, I was on uniformed duty in an unmarked police cruiser assigned to the Administration Section, working from 7:00 a.m.-3:30 p.m. At approximately 12:44 p.m., I was operating my cruiser on Harvard Street near West Street. At that time, I overheard an ECC broadcast for a possible break-in in progress at West Street. Due to my proximity, I responded.

When I arrived at West Street, I radioed ECC and asked that they have the caller meet me at the front door to this residence. I was told that the caller was already outside. As I was getting this information, I climbed the porch stairs toward the front door. As I reached the door, a female voice called out to me. I turned and looked in the direction of the voice and observed a white female, later identified as Kate Lander. Lander, who was standing on the sidewalk in front of the residence, held a wireless telephone in her hand and told me that it was she who called. She went on to tell me that she observed what appeared to be two black males with backpacks on the porch of West Street. She told me that her suspicions were aroused when she observed one of the men wedging his shoulder into the door as if he was trying to force entry. Since I was the only police officer on location and had my back to the front door as I spoke with her, I asked that she wait for other responding officers while I investigated further.

As I turned and faced the door, I could see an older black male standing in the foyer of West Street. I made this observation through the glass paned front door.

As I stood in plain view of this man, later identified as Matthew, I asked if he would step out onto the porch and speak with me. He replied "no I will not." He then demanded to know who I was. I told him that I was "Sgt. Smith from the Cambridge Police" and that I was "investigating a report of break-in in progress" at the residence. While I was making this statement, Matthew opened the front door and exclaimed "why, because I'm a black man in America?" I then asked Matthew if there was anyone else in the residence. While yelling, he told me that it was none of my business and accused me of being a racist police officer. I assured Matthew that I was responding to a citizen's call to the Cambridge Police and that the caller was outside as we spoke. Matthew seemed to ignore me and picked up a cordless telephone and dialed an unknown telephone number. As he did so, I radioed on channel 1 that I was off in the residence with someone who appeared to be a resident but very uncooperative. I then overheard Matthew asking the person at the other end of his telephone call to "get the chief" and "what's the chief's name?" Matthew was telling the person on the other end of the call that he was dealing with a racist police officer in his home. Matthew then turned to me and told me that I had no idea who I was "messing" with and that I had not heard the last of it. While I was led to believe that Matthew was lawfully in the residence, I was quite surprised and confused with the behavior he exhibited toward me. I asked Matthew to provide me with photo identification so that I could verify that he resided at West Street and so that I could radio my findings to ECC. Matthew initially refused, demanding that I show him identification, but then did supply me with a Harvard University identification card. Upon learning that Matthew was affiliated with Harvard, I radioed and requested the presence of the Harvard University Police.

With the Harvard University identification in hand, I radioed my findings to ECC on channel two and prepared to leave. Matthew again asked for my name, which I began to provide. Matthew began to yell over my spoken words by accusing me of being a racist police officer and leveling threats that he wasn't someone to mess with. At some point during this exchange, I became aware that Off. Carlos Figueroa was standing behind me. When Matthew asked a third time for my name, I explained to him that I had provided it at his request two separate times. Matthew continued to yell at me. I told Matthew that I was leaving his residence and that if he had any other questions regarding the matter, I would speak with him outside of the residence.

As I began walking through the foyer toward the front door, I could hear Matthew again demanding my name. I again told Matthew that I would speak with him outside. My reason for wanting to leave the residence was that Matthew was yelling very loud and the acoustics of the kitchen and foyer were making it difficult for me to transmit pertinent information to ECC or other responding units. His reply was "Ya, I'll speak with your mama outside." When I left the residence, I noted that there were several Cambridge and Harvard University police officers assembled on the sidewalk in front of the residence.

Additionally, the caller, Ms. Lander, and at least seven unidentified passers-by were looking in the direction of Matthew, who had followed me outside of the residence.

As I descended the stairs to the sidewalk, Matthew continued to yell at me, accusing me of racial bias and continued to tell me that I had not heard the last of him. Due to the tumultuous manner Matthew had exhibited in his residence as well as his continued tumultuous behavior outside the residence, in view of the public, I warned Matthew that he was becoming disorderly. Matthew ignored my warning and continued to yell, which drew the attention of both the police officers and citizens, who appeared surprised and alarmed by Matthew's outburst. For a second time, I warned Matthew to calm down while I withdrew my department issued handcuffs from their carrying case. Matthew again ignored my warning and continued to yell at me. It was at this time that I informed Matthew that he was under arrest. I then stepped up the stairs, onto the porch and attempted to place handcuffs on Matthew. Matthew initially resisted my attempt to handcuff him, yelling that he was "disabled" and would fall without his cane. After the handcuffs were properly applied, Matthew complained that they were too tight. I ordered Off. Green, who was among the responding officers, to handcuff Matthew with his arms in front of him for his comfort while I secured a cane for Matthew from within the residence. I then asked Matthew if he would like an officer to take possession of his house key and secure his front door, which he left wide open. Matthew told me that the door was unsecurable due to a previous break-in attempt at the residence. Shortly thereafter, a Harvard maintenance person arrived on scene and appeared familiar with Matthew. I asked Matthew if he was comfortable with this Harvard University maintenance person securing his residence. He told me that he was.

After a brief consultation with Sgt. Lester and upon Matthew's request, he was transported to 125 6th Street in a police cruiser (Car 1, Off.'s Rosenthal and Green) where he was booked and processed by Off. J.P. Smith.

Cambridge Police
SUPPLEMENTAL REPORT #2256-2

Date: July 19, 2014
Place: West St.
Incident Type/Offense: Disorderly Conduct c272 S53
Reporting Officer: Alphonse DeNato

Offender: Lincoln Matthew, Jr.
Sex: Male
Race: Black
Age: 58

Narrative

On July 17, 2014 at approximately 12:44 p.m., I, Officer DeNato #509 responded to an ECC broadcast for a possible break-in at West St. When I arrived, I stepped into the residence and Sgt. Smith had already entered and was speaking to a black male.

As I stepped in, I heard Sgt. Smith ask for the gentleman's information to which he stated "NO I WILL NOT!"

The gentleman was shouting out to the Sgt. that the Sgt. was a racist and yelled that "THIS IS WHAT HAPPENS TO BLACK MEN IN AMERICA!" As the Sgt. was trying to calm the gentleman, the gentleman shouted "YOU DON'T KNOW WHO YOU'RE MESSING WITH!"

I stepped out to gather the information from the reporting person, LANDER, KATE. Ms. Lander stated to me that she saw a man wedging his shoulder into the front door as to pry the door open. As I returned to the residence, a group of onlookers were now on scene. The Sgt. along with the gentleman, were now on the porch of West St. and again he was shouting, now to the onlookers (about seven), "THIS IS WHAT HAPPENS TO BLACK MEN IN AMERICA!" The gentleman refused to listen to as to why the Cambridge Police were there.

While on the porch, the gentleman refused to be cooperative and continued shouting that the Sgt. is a racist police officer.

911 OPERATOR: 9-1-1, what is the exact location of your emergency?

FEMALE WITNESS CALLER: Hi, I'm actually at (inaudible) street in Cambridge, the house number is 7 West Street.

911 OPERATOR: OK, ma'am, your cell phone cut out, what's the address again?

FEMALE WITNESS CALLER: Sorry, it's 7 West Street. That's W-E-S-T Street.

911 OPERATOR: The emergency is at 7 West Street, right?

FEMALE WITNESS CALLER: Well no, I'm sorry. 17. Some other woman is talking next to me but it's 17, 1-7 West Street.

911 OPERATOR: What's the phone number you're calling me from?

FEMALE WITNESS CALLER: I'm calling you from my cell phone number.

911 OPERATOR: All right, tell me exactly what happened?

FEMALE WITNESS CALLER: Um, I don't know what's happening. I just had an older woman standing here and she had noticed two gentlemen trying to get in a house at that number, 17 West Street. And they kind of had to barge in and they broke the screen door and they finally got in. When I had looked, I went further, closer to the house a little bit after the gentlemen were already in the house. I noticed two suitcases. So, I'm not sure if this is two individuals who actually work there, I mean, who live there.

911 OPERATOR: You think they might have been breaking in?

FEMALE WITNESS CALLER: I don't know 'cause I have no idea. I just noticed.

911 OPERATOR: So you're saying you think the possibility might have been there? What do you mean by barged in? You mean they kicked the door in?

FEMALE WITNESS CALLER: No, they were pushing the door in. Like, umm, the screen part of the front door was kind of like cut.

911 OPERATOR: How did they open the door itself with the lock?

FEMALE WITNESS CALLER: They, I didn't see a key or anything 'cause I was a little bit away from the door. But I did notice that they pushed their (interrupted).

911 OPERATOR: And what do the suitcases have to do with anything?

FEMALE WITNESS CALLER: I don't know, I'm just saying that's what I saw.

911 OPERATOR: Do you know what apartment they broke into?

FEMALE WITNESS CALLER: No, they're just the first floor. I don't even think that it's an apartment. It's 17 West Street. It's a house, it's a yellow house. Number 17. I don't know if they live there and they just had a hard time with their key but I did notice that they kind of used their shoulder to kind of barge in and they got in. I don't know if they had a key or not because I couldn't see from my angle. But, you know, when I looked a little closely that's what I saw.

911 OPERATOR: (inaudible) guy or Hispanic?

FEMALE WITNESS CALLER: Umm.

911 OPERATOR: Are they still in the house?

FEMALE WITNESS CALLER: They're still in the house, I believe, yeah.

911 OPERATOR: Were they white, black, or Hispanic?

FEMALE WITNESS CALLER: Umm, well there were two larger men, one looked kind of Hispanic but I'm not really sure. And the other one entered and I didn't see what he looked like at all. I just saw it from a distance and this older woman was worried thinking someone's breaking in someone's house, they've been barging in. And she interrupted me and that's when I had noticed otherwise I probably wouldn't have noticed it at all, to be honest with you. So, I was just calling 'cause she was a concerned neighbor, I guess.

911 OPERATOR: OK, are you standing outside?

FEMALE WITNESS CALLER: I'm standing outside, yes.

911 OPERATOR: All right, the police are on the way, you can meet them when they get there. What's your name?

FEMALE WITNESS CALLER: Yeah, my name is (deleted).

911 OPERATOR: All right, we're on the way.

FEMALE WITNESS CALLER: OK. All right, I guess I'll wait. Thanks.

B. UNDERSTAND THE FACTS OF MATTHEW'S CASE

For case file 1, the facts were given to you in a single memo. Here, you will need to gather the facts from a few sources: the police reports and the 911 transcript. The newspaper reports give you a context for what happened, but the facts contained therein may not be reliable, so you should not use them as a basis for your legal analysis.

Review the police reports and the 911 transcript and make notes. Until you have read the statute and the authority you won't know exactly which facts are going to be critical, but you will have a good understanding of what happened to our client. Later, once you know what the rules are and how the courts have applied the rules in other circumstances, you will come back to the facts and evaluate which ones are critical to the outcome of the case (the decisive facts).

Case file 2 contains a few documents from which you will have to discern the important facts. Effective lawyering will require that you keep careful notes of client and witness interviews and phone calls, as well as organized notes of what is in the client's file. A client's file can be voluminous. Most law offices will have a method for keeping track of file contents. As you proceed through law school and in your summer jobs and internships, you will be exposed to these methods and will become accustomed to the practice.

At this stage, you will develop your own practice of keeping clear notes on the contents of a client's file. Case file 2 is not voluminous by any stretch, but it is a good place to start becoming an effective note taker.

1. An Approach to Note Taking

Here is a suggested step-by-step approach to note taking, but you will likely personalize how you take notes as you gain more experience:

- Read the entire file
- Organize the documents logically (either chronologically, or by subject or witness)

A suggested note-taking structure:

Who: Identify all the key players in the case and note why the person is a key player. For example, in the Matthew case the key players are Professor Matthew, Officer Crowley, the caller, and the group of onlookers.

What: The "What" contains two parts. First, note what each document is. For example, in the Matthew case, the police reports will form the basis of our analysis, but the newspaper reports carry less weight as the information is less reliable. In the same way, a deposition made under oath is reliable whereas a news report is less so. Second, make notes on what happened. For example, in the Matthew case the notes might begin with the caller reporting a break-in at Matthew's home. Go on to chronicle what happened next. As you make these notes, identify where each piece of information comes from.

Where: This identifies the geographic location of the client's problem.

When: This is a timeline of key dates or times that are relevant to your client's case. Depending on the case, one or more of these categories will vary in importance. Sometimes the dates and times that certain events took place are the most critical aspect of a case. In that situation your timeline will be more developed than in a case where, for example, the case turns on a set of specific facts as in the Potter case.

CASE FILE 2: Assignment—Review Facts from the Matthew File

Write up notes on the Matthew file following the Who, What, Where, When format.

2. Read and Study Relevant Statute and Cases

Once you have obtained all the cases listed in case file 2 along with the statute, you will apply the methods you learned in doing case file 1:

- Read and brief each case
- Read and outline the statute
- Identify the relevant elements in the statute (i.e., the ones that apply to the Matthew case)

The Matthew case requires that you analyze the Massachusetts Disorderly Conduct Statute. For case file 1, you learned how to break the statute down, but the assignment identified which of the DUI elements you had to analyze. For case file 2, you will need to study the Disorderly Conduct Statute as it applies to the Matthew case. You will also have to predict if his actions constitute a violation of the statute. What follows is a review of how to read and outline a statute. This review should help you decipher the Disorderly Conduct Statute.

Remember from Chapter 3 that legislatures can make it difficult to easily identify the elements that make up a statutory violation. It would be useful if every statute looked like this:

Violating the Burglary Statute requires the following elements:

- breaking and entering
- into a dwelling
- with the intent to commit a misdemeanor therein

Unfortunately, many statutes do not break down the elements so clearly and thus we are left to dissect the statute and figure out what elements make up a violation or a cause of action.

Let's examine a statute in the context of a client who is bitten by a dog. Imagine that your client, a 16-year-old girl, was bitten by a dog after she let herself into her friend's house to retrieve her iPod that she had left there by accident. She had let herself in many times in the past, as she knew where the family kept the hide-a-key. The family was aware that she had done this and never objected. On this occasion, she startled the dog and he bit her in the leg causing a deep cut.

Here is what the state Dog Bite Statute says:

> The owner of any dog which shall bite a person while such person is on or in a public place, or lawfully on or in a private place including the property of the owner of the dog, shall be liable for such damages as may be suffered by the person bitten, regardless of the former viciousness of such dog or the owner's knowledge of such viciousness.

Your first step is to identify what you must show in order to make a viable complaint against the family. To be viable, you would have to show that all requirements of the statute have been met.

So let's break it down:

[The owner of any dog] – *This tells you who can violate the statute.*

[which shall bite a person] – *This tells you what act the statute prohibits.*

[while such person is on or in a public place or lawfully on or in a private place, including the property of the owner of the dog,] – *This tells you the circumstances that must be present for a violation of the statute.*

[shall be liable for such damages as may be suffered by the person bitten] – *This tells you that the owner <u>will</u> be liable, which means that this is a strict liability statute. The state of mind of the owner does not matter.*

[regardless of the former viciousness of the dog or the owner's knowledge of such viciousness.] – *This tells you that the dog owner has no defense to the violation if he or she was unaware of the dog's propensity to violence.*

The basic requirements, or elements, are that:

- The defendant is the owner of the dog.
- The dog bit the plaintiff.
- The bite happened when the plaintiff was in or on a public place or was lawfully in or on a private place.

Very often a court will have already gone through this process and identified the elements of a statute. Once you know what statute or statutes you are dealing with, the next step is to see if the courts have addressed the elements of the statute. For example, if the above set of facts had occurred in New Jersey, you could have researched the Dog Bite Statute and discovered this case:

Devito v. Anderson, 410 N.J.Super. 175, 980 A.2d 498 (2009)

(Excerpted)

Plaintiffs Sandra DeVivo and John DeVivo ("DeVivos") bring this motion before the court seeking summary judgment as to liability against defendants Britney Anderson and Suzanne Anderson ("Andersons"). Plaintiffs allege that the Andersons are strictly liable pursuant to N.J.S.A. 4:19-16, the so called "dog bite" statute, for Sandra DeVivo's injuries. Sandra contends that Suzanne Anderson's German Shepherd dog, Magic, bit her on the forearm as she was walking past the front of defendants' residence. At the time Magic was unleashed. Britney, Suzanne's daughter, was holding on to Magic by his collar. Also before the court is defendants' cross-motion for summary judgment. Defendants contend that Sandra cannot meet the statutory requirements of N.J.S.A. 4:19-16 since "there was no broken skin or evidence of any type of bite caused ..." by Magic. Defendants' notice of motion also seeks summary judgment with respect to plaintiffs' common law negligence cause of action.

...*N.J.S.A.* 4:19-16 imposes strict liability upon an owner whose dog bites another, without proof of the owner's knowledge of the dog's vicious propensities. The "dog bite" statute states:

> The owner of any dog which shall bite a person while such person is on or in a public place, or lawfully on or in a private place including the property of the owner of the dog, shall be liable for such damages as may be suffered by the person bitten, regardless of the former vicious-ness of such dog or the owner's knowledge of such viciousness.

Thus, "[t]he three elements plaintiff must prove under *N.J.S.A.* 4:19-16 are that: (1) defendant is the owner of the dog; (2) the dog bit plaintiff; and (3) the bite occurred while the plaintiff was either in a public place or lawfully in a private place." *Trisuzzi v. Tabatchnik*, 285 N.J.Super. 15, 23, 666 A.2d 543 (App.Div.1995).

In the instant matter, there is no dispute as to the first and third elements. Defendant, Suzanne Anderson, admits that she is Magic's owner and that plaintiff, Sandra DeVivo, was in a public place when the incident occurred. With respect to the second element, the parties dispute whether a "dog bite" occurred sufficient to meet the requirements of N.J.S.A. 4:19-16. Defendants argue that no bite occurred because, based on the hospital reports, there was no broken skin or any evidence of any type of a bite. Defendants point to the assessment/treatment notes in Sandra's hospital records which state "right arm swelling noted. Skin intact. No broken/open areas noted." Defendants further contend that there is no evidence as to the cause of the bruising on Sandra's arm and deny that the photographs of Sandra's injuries depict bruising on her right arm resulting from Magic's teeth. Defendants conceded at oral argument that there may be circumstances in which a "bite" may occur despite the fact that no tearing of the skin occurred. However, under these circumstances, defendants argue Sandra was not bitten by Magic.

The court tells you what the elements are. Here the issue centers on the "bite" element, but not what it means to be lawfully on another's property. For our client, we would have to research cases that discuss this particular element to find out if our client has a viable clam.

CASE FILE 2: Assignment—Identify the Elements of the Massachusetts Disorderly Conduct Statute

CHAPTER 11

A Closer Look at Hierarchy of Authority in Context

In Chapter 4 we reviewed the concept of Weight of Authority. Now we will look more closely at how to use cases to solve a legal problem when those cases come from different court levels. Remember, your mission is to give a well-reasoned and thorough answer to the legal problem raised in the case. Finding the authority is step one (here that has been done for you). The next step is to figure out how you will use the authority to best explain your conclusion. The Matthew case involves a Massachusetts state law, so our focus will be mainly on state court decisions. However, there is one federal case in our list of cases, so we will need to figure out how that fits into the hierarchy of cases.

First, let's take a closer look at how state courts are structured. Most states have several levels of courts. Generally, at the lowest level is the trial court, above that is an intermediary court, and at the top is the highest

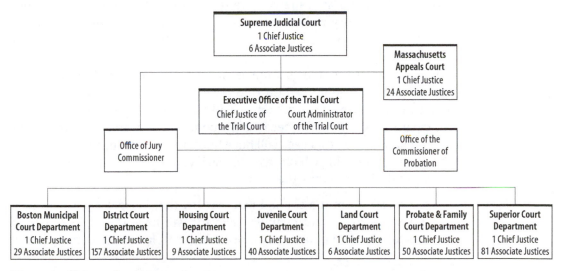

Diagram of Massachusetts court system.

appellate court. Often, there are specialized courts at the lowest level, such as family courts or probate courts. For example, on the previous page is an image of the Massachusetts court system taken from the State Court Web site.[1] Notice that there is a Supreme Judicial Court, an Appeals Court, and, at the lower level, several different types of trial courts.

Remember, every state's system is different. Some states do not have a mid-level appellate court. In those states, all appeals go directly to the highest court. Some states, like New York, have confusing names for courts. New York's highest court is titled the Court of Appeals and one of the lowest courts (at the trial level) is titled Supreme Courts.

PRACTICAL TIP

There are two helpful and easily accessible resources for figuring out a state's court structure. First, in the back of the *Bluebook* or *ALWD* there is a table of citations for states. You can easily identify the court levels (and proper citation) in these tables. You can also look at a state's official court Web site. These Web sites typically have a chart or explanation of the different court levels.

Typically, only the appeals court opinions are officially reported. When you are researching a legal problem you will mainly study appellate court opinions; however, there may be opinions or orders from lower courts that you want to look at and use. State lower court opinions and orders may be available online or in hard copy at the courthouse. They will be more difficult to find, but WestlawNext does have lower court orders in some cases. You may also find relevant lower court orders by talking with other practitioners who may know about a particular case where the judge wrote an order addressing an issue you are researching. These opinions do not carry any mandatory weight with other judges, but they may have some persuasive weight, particularly if your case is before a court at a similar or lower level.

If the answer to your legal issue lies in several cases, some from a state's highest court and some from a mid-level court, how will you use these cases to explain your answer? Cases will be useful to you either because they clearly set out a rule or because the court applies facts that are similar to your client's. The best cases will have both: relevant facts and clear rules. When you are choosing which cases to use if your case is in state court, here is a way to decide and rank them,

> ***Best:*** A case from the state's highest court that is legally (i.e., the case gives the rules) and factually relevant will have the highest weight because it is mandatory authority, highly relevant, and very useful.

---

1. http://www.mass.gov/courts/court-info/about-mass-courts/

You may use a case like this both in your roadmap paragraph and in your explanation and application of the law.

Good: A case from the state's highest court that clearly sets out a relevant rule but does not have similar facts will be useful in giving the rule, but not necessarily useful in justifying your factual conclusion. You could use a case like this in your roadmap paragraph, but not in your explanation and application of the law.

Good: A case from a mid-level appeals court that clearly sets out a relevant rule and where the court compares similar facts to your client's will be useful even though it is not mandatory authority. Your audience (whether it is another lawyer, a client, or a judge) will benefit and be persuaded by knowing that another court applied facts just like your client's and came to the same conclusion you are advancing.

Good: A case from a different jurisdiction or from the federal system (if you are handling a problem in state court) that applies a similar rule to facts that are similar to your client's. Federal courts will hear cases involving state law, such as those that come before them under diversity jurisdiction[2] or federal claims that require resolution of a state law in reaching a result. These cases are not mandatory authority because they are decided under a different court system, however, they can be persuasive. U.S. Supreme Court cases would be included here. Even though the case is from the highest Court in the country, it is not mandatory to a state court.

Helpful: Trial court orders, particularly from a parallel trial court, can be persuasive though not binding. For example, if your case is in a state trial court and a judge from another trial court in a different county had written an order or opinion about the identical issue you are addressing, the opinion or order may help persuade the judge you are in front of that your position is correct. The trick is finding the orders because often they are not reported and the only record of the opinion will be a copy in the court's file. Some electronic databases now include state trial court orders (such as WestlawNext). Depending on the local rules of the jurisdiction you are in, you may need to append a copy to your motion or memorandum so the reader will have access to the opinion. Federal trial court orders are recorded on F. Supp. and online at Google Scholar.

Helpful: Unpublished opinions have not been officially reported but have nevertheless been recorded, often in an electronic database such as Google Scholar, Westlaw, or Lexis, or in their own reporter (the Federal Appendix). Unpublished federal opinions can also be found on court Web sites or on Pacer. Thus, you can find them, however,

---

2. Generally, diversity jurisdiction is where the parties in a lawsuit are from different states or are non-U.S. citizens.

they are officially labeled as "unpublished." In the early 1970s, the judiciary sought to limit the number of published opinions because of the growth in appellate cases. Both to limit creation of "bad law" coming out of frivolous cases, and to reduce workloads, the courts decided that unpublished opinions would have no precedential value and, thus, theoretically take less time to write. However, some courts allow use of unpublished opinions. You can find out whether the court you are in permits them by checking the court rules for the state. Federal Rule of Appellate Procedure 32.1 requires federal courts to permit nonprecedential opinions to be cited with some restrictions.

The date of an opinion is relevant to its precedential value. Newer cases that give the same rule are better than older ones because they alert the reader that the rule is recent and still good. When a precedent is found in a very old case and in a new one, giving both cites can be useful to show that the rule has a history. There is an example of this on page 93. Notice the age of the *Dow* case that is cited with the *Vodra* case.

CASE FILE 2: Assignment—Review the Cases in the Matthew Case

Identify the weight of each case used to support the Matthew case.

CHAPTER 12

Developing the Rules in a Multi-Issue Case

Remember that for case file 1 you synthesized a rule for a single issue from three cases. For case file 2 you will be using the same strategies, but applying them to more cases and issues. You may want to start by making a chart for each issue similar to the chart you made for case file 1. This may seem overwhelming at first. Organizing with a chart or some other visual tool will help you tame the information, as shown below.

Element	*Sholley*	*Lopiano*	*Mulvey*	*Levine*	Commonalities
	Decisive facts: Holding/ Reasoning:	Decisive facts: Holding/ Reasoning:	Decisive facts: Holding/ Reasoning:	Decisive facts: Holding/ Reasoning:	
	Decisive facts: Holding/ Reasoning:	Decisive facts: Holding/ Reasoning:	Decisive facts: Holding/ Reasoning:	Decisive facts: Holding/ Reasoning:	

Once you have identified the commonalities for each element you can develop a synthesized rule for each of the elements. These rules will be the anchor for your discussion on each element. You have completed this type of exercise for case file 1 using one element (whether or not the client was driving). For case file 2, you will essentially write two synthesized rules and two discussions, one for each element that you have to explain.

CASE FILE 2: Assignment—Write a Rule

Write a rule pertaining to each element that you must explain in the Matthew case.

A multi-element memo must start with an overall roadmap paragraph that gives the reader an introduction of what is to come in the discussion section. Then you will write a "mini roadmap" that pertains to each element. Here is an example of an overall roadmap in a Massachusetts memo that explains the law on when custodial interrogations trigger the requirement of Miranda warnings:

Conclusion sentence

Introduction of the overall rule

Break down of the issues (here they are factors)

Connor can likely show that he was subjected to a custodial interrogation by the Newbury chief of police in the absence of adequate Miranda warnings. Miranda warnings are necessary for "custodial interrogations." *Miranda v. Arizona,* 384 U.S. 436, 444 (1966). Custodial interrogation is questioning initiated by law enforcement officers after a person has been taken into custody or otherwise deprived of his freedom of action in any significant way. *Id.* There are four factors that determine whether an individual's freedom of action is sufficiently curtailed such that Miranda warnings are required: (1) the place of the interrogation; (2) whether the investigation has begun to focus on the suspect, including whether there is probable cause to arrest the suspect; (3) the nature of the interrogation, including whether the interview was aggressive or, instead, informal and influenced in its contours by the suspect; and (4) whether, at the time the incriminating statement was made, the suspect was free to end the interview by leaving the locus of the interrogation or by asking the interrogator to leave, as evidenced by whether the interview terminated with the defendant's arrest. *Commonwealth v. Bryant,* 390 Mass. 729, 737 (1984). No one factor is conclusive. *Commonwealth vs. Bryant,* 390 Mass. 729 (1984). Nor is there a specific formula to be applied. *Commonwealth vs. Haas,* 373 Mass. 545 (1977).

The remainder of the discussion section will be organized around each of the four factors. A reader-friendly way to alert your reader that you will be explaining each sub-issue individually is to divide the sections of the discussion into parts that have brief headings. Here the headings could be:

1. Place of Interrogation
2. Focus of Investigation
3. Nature of Investigation
4. Suspect's Freedom to Leave

Each of the subsections will begin with a mini-roadmap paragraph that gives the reader the rule on the sub-issue.

EXAMPLE: Place of Interrogation

Conclusion on sub-issue

Rule on sub-issue

Although Connor's questioning occurred in his apartment, the court may still find that this rose to "custodial interrogation" because there were six uniformed police officers present at the time. Courts are concerned with interrogations that take place in a police-dominated atmosphere. *Commonwealth v. Shine,* 398 Mass 641, 648 (1986). See *Miranda, supra,* at 445. Although it is less likely that the circumstances are custodial when the interrogation occurs in familiar surroundings, the courts will examine whether "a reasonable person in the defendant's circumstances would have found the setting isolating and coercive." *Breese v. Commonwealth,* 415 Mass. 249, 255 (1993); *Commonwealth v. Gallati,* 40 Mass. App. Ct. 111, 113 (1996).

> ### PRACTICAL TIP
>
> For an interoffice memo, headings of subsections should be brief. Although lawyers may have particular formats for writing headings, generally it is most helpful to the reader if the heading is one to three words. Think of headings as signposts written to alert the reader about which part of the overall rule the section will address.

The paragraphs that follow each mini-roadmap will further explain the rule by using case illustrations or rule-based reasoning, as appropriate, and application of the law to the client's facts.

Here is a visual of how the discussion paragraphs in a multi-issue interoffice objective memo could be organized:

Discussion

Overall roadmap: sets out overall rule, including sub-issues. These might be elements, factors, or distinct parts of a rule.

Heading: Sub-Element 1

Mini-roadmap of sub-element 1: sets out rule pertaining to element, factor, or distinct part.

Explanation of sub-element 1. This may take more than one paragraph depending on how many cases you need to use to illustrate the rule, or how complex the sub-issue is.

Application of sub-element 1. As with the explanation paragraphs, this may take more than one paragraph depending on how many cases you need to use to illustrate the rule, or how complex the sub-issue is.

Heading: Sub-Element 2

Mini-roadmap of sub-element 2: sets out rule pertaining to element, factor, or distinct part.

Explanation of sub-element 2. This may take more than one paragraph depending on how many cases you need to use to illustrate the rule, or how complex the sub-issue is.

Application of sub-element 2. As with the explanation paragraphs, this may take more than one paragraph depending on how many cases you need to use to illustrate the rule, or how complex the sub-issue is.

CHAPTER 13

Counter-Analysis

The purpose of a counter-analysis is to let your reader know what the potential weaknesses are in your prediction and how you will address them. You should always have an idea about what the opposing counsel might argue, or what a court might have concerns about. The counter-analysis lets your reader know that you have looked at the law from all angles and have ideas about how to approach weaknesses. Including a counter-analysis will give your reader assurance that your thinking is thorough, deep, and has left no stone unturned.

A counter-analysis usually fits in at the end of an application. Here is the counter-analysis in the sample memo on page 9.

> Albert's only argument in her favor likely relies on the underlying purpose of 404(b). She could argue that allowing the bad act evidence against her goes against the purpose behind 404(b) and its limitations. *Id.* at 1195 (holding purpose underlying rule 404(b) is to ensure that a defendant is tried on the merits of the case and not on character). However, the concern that a defendant not be convicted on the basis of character is met where, as here, there is a sufficient, specific purpose for its admission. By claiming that she mistakenly took the ham, Albert's placed her own intent to commit theft at issue. The prosecutor would probably be successful in arguing that the purpose of the evidence is to refute that claim and not to demonstrate her bad character.

Notice that the first sentence alerts the reader specifically that the writer is addressing weaknesses or opposing arguments. Then the potential argument is laid out followed by the legal foundation that might support it. Next the writer explains how and why the counter-argument is unlikely to succeed.

Here is another example of a counter-analysis. In this case, imagine that you are working for a prosecutor and you've been asked to write a memo predicting whether a defendant, who is charged with gun possession, can successfully move to suppress the gun on grounds that it was recovered by the police after an illegal stop and search. After researching the law, you have concluded that the police probably acted lawfully. This is the discussion section of the memo:

Overall roadmap paragraph

The police likely acted reasonably under art. 14 of the Massachusetts Constitution and the Fourth Amendment where they made a limited pat frisk of Carter after receiving information that Carter "displayed" a firearm at an after hours party and yelled to bystanders he would be back. Under art. 14 of the Massachusetts Constitution and the Fourth Amendment, police officers act reasonably when they stop and frisk a suspect after receiving information that the suspect is in possession of a firearm when the circumstances indicate a concern for public safety. *Commonwealth v. Foster*, 724 N.E.2d 357, 361 (Mass. App. Ct. 2000). An informant's report that a suspect is carrying a gun, without any other indicia of danger to police or the public, is not enough to justify a stop and frisk. *Commonwealth v. Couture*, 552 N.E.2d 538, 540 (Mass. 1990). However, when the circumstances give rise to public safety concerns, the police have a duty to investigate a tip of gun possession "and may perform a pat frisk if they have a reasonable belief that the defendant is 'armed and dangerous.'" *Foster*, 724 N.E.2d at 359-60.

Explanation of the law with examples

Massachusetts courts have upheld a suspect's stop and pat frisk where the tip came from a known or anonymous source and the information involved firearms possession under circumstances indicating the suspect presented a danger to public safety. *Commonwealth v. Johnson*, 631 N.E.2d 71, 72 (Mass. App. Ct. 1994*); Commonwealth v. McCauley*, 419 N.E.2d 1072, 1073 (Mass. App. Ct. 1981). For example, in *Johnson*, the court upheld a pat frisk where a known citizen informed police a suspect was carrying a gun, and the suspect was shouting obscenities and gesticulating in an angry manner. 631 N.E.2d at 72. In *McCauley*, the court upheld a pat frisk based on an anonymous tip where the suspect was in a well-filled café at a late hour, may have been intoxicated, and had dropped his firearm repeatedly on the floor. 419 N.E.2d at 1073. The McCauley court noted that "the [late] hour, the location of the inquiry, the risks to other patrons, and the specificity of the anonymous report describing McCauley" justified the police officers' actions. *Id.*

Explanation of the law with examples

Reasonableness is at the center of any art. 14 of the Massachusetts Constitution or Fourth Amendment analysis regarding governmental intrusion of a person's body. *Id.* Where, as in *Johnson* and *McCauley*, the suspects by their conduct and manner presented a danger to others, the police had a duty to investigate a tip regarding firearm possession from a known informant or, as in *McCauley*, from an anonymous informant where the tip was specific enough to warrant reliance upon it. *Johnson*, 631 N.E.2d at 72; *McCauley*, 419 N.E.2d at 1073. Thus, the police acted reasonably in both cases when they performed a limited pat frisk of each of the defendants to uncover a weapon. *Johnson*, 631 N.E.2d at 72; *McCauley*, 419 N.E.2d at 1073.

Explanation of the law with examples

If the informant's tip merely informs police that a suspect possesses a firearm, without an indication of a threat or risk to the public, a stop and frisk is not justified. *Couture*, 552 N.E.2d at 541. In *Couture*, a store clerk called police and informed them that a customer had entered his store and "had a small handgun protruding from his right rear pocket." *Id.* at 539. Police subsequently stopped the customer based on the clerk's report of the customer's license plate, ordered him out of his truck, searched his vehicle, and discovered a .38 caliber pistol under the front seat. *Id.* In suppressing the evidence, the court reasoned the tip provided no evidence that the customer acted suspiciously in the store. *Id.* at 540. He did not threaten or intimidate the clerk; nor did he linger suspiciously or act like he was "casing the joint" in order to commit a robbery. *Id.* The only information police knew from the tip was that the customer possessed a gun in a public place. *Id.* As a result, without more, the officers' stop and seizure of the defendant, his vehicle, and his gun was unlawful where nothing indicated the customer was about to engage in illegal activity. *Id.* at 541.

Here the police likely acted reasonably when they pat frisked Carter based on the known informant's tip because the circumstances surrounding the tip likely indicated that Carter posed a threat to public safety. Like the *McCauley* case, where the police received a tip that *McCauley* had displayed a firearm late at night when he may have been intoxicated, Carter displayed a firearm in public after leaving a party in the early morning. The police in *Johnson* also acted reasonably in pat frisking the defendant after receiving a tip from a known informant that she was carrying a gun and acting belligerently. Similarly, the police here acted reasonably in pat frisking Carter because he "displayed" a firearm at an early morning hour and yelled to bystanders that he would be back. In fact, the police had a duty to investigate here, just like in the precedent cases, because the circumstances, including the defendant's conduct and the early hour, indicated a threat to public safety. Like the police officers in *Johnson* and *McCauley*, who acted reasonably under the circumstances when they made a limited pat frisk of individuals who posed a threat to the public, the police likely acted reasonably here and complied with art. 14 of the Massachusetts Constitution and the Fourth Amendment when they made a limited pat frisk of Carter based on information from a known informant that he posed a threat to public safety.

Application of the law

Carter may argue that his case is like *Couture* in that there was no information other than his public possession of a firearm without any threat. This would make the stop and frisk unreasonable under the circumstances and a violation of his rights under art. 14 of the Massachusetts Constitution and the Fourth Amendment. This argument will likely fail. In *Couture*, other than the store clerk's statement that he saw the customer with a gun, there existed no additional indicia that created a concern for public safety. As the court noted in *Couture*, despite wearing the gun on his person, the defendant did not act suspiciously in the store. In *McCauley*, the court relied on "the [late] hour, the location of the inquiry, the risks to other patrons, and the specificity of the anonymous report describing McCauley" to justify the police officers' actions. Similarly, in the instant case, the hour was late, there were several people still at the party when Carter displayed his weapon and indicated he would be back, and the tip from the informant described what Carter was wearing and in which direction he had headed after leaving the party.

Counter-analysis

Effective Counter-Analysis—Do's and Don'ts
- Use words or phrases to alert the reader that you are shifting to the counter-analysis. In the example above, the writer does this by saying, "Carter may argue that..."

- Be specific about the factual basis and legal grounds for a counter-analysis.

  Not helpful: Carter may argue that the police acted unreasonably in stopping and frisking him.

  Helpful: Carter may argue that his case is like *Couture*, and that there was no information other than his public possession of a firearm without any threat. This would make the stop and frisk unreasonable under the circumstances and a violation of his rights under art. 14 of the Massachusetts Constitution and the Fourth Amendment.
- Include the legal support for the counter-analysis. Notice in the example above that the writer shows how the *Couture* case could be used for supporting a different legal conclusion.
- Specifically refute the counter-analysis. Show the reader how you would deal with the opposing position. In the example above, the reader is clear about this when she says, "This argument will likely fail." She follows this with the specific reasons why it will fail.

Lawyering often requires advocating for a particular position. Usually there will be an opposing position. An effective lawyer can anticipate opposing arguments. You will need to feel comfortable stepping into the shoes of opposing counsel to see the legal issue from a different perspective. Even as you advocate zealously for your client.

Let's return to our client in Chapter 6, the one who was arrested for texting while she walked down a sidewalk. Recall that she was looking up directions on her iPhone and not actually texting with another individual. Based on an analysis of the three cases, it looked like she did not violate the statute because she was not communicating with another person. However, what if you were the prosecutor in the case? Would you have a different interpretation? How would you argue that the defendant had violated the statute? If you were asked to draft a memo for your supervisor that analyzed whether the defendant violated the statute, you would include a section that addressed the likely arguments that the prosecutor might make. You would also address how you would meet those arguments.

CASE FILE 2: Assignment—Practice Writing a Counter-Analysis

Write a brief (one paragraph) counter-analysis explaining what the prosecutor would likely argue in the texting case on page 68. Include why that argument would not prevail.

PART IV

CASE FILE 3
Berger v. Photo Restorations, LLC

CHAPTER 14

Introduction to Case File 3

Case file 3 involves an issue about personal jurisdiction. You will recognize the legal concepts from your civil procedure class. Here you will be asked to find out how advertising and doing business over the Internet impacts decisions regarding a court's jurisdiction over a legal matter. Your familiarity with personal jurisdiction will give you a good base for researching and applying the law in a South Dakota case.

Case file 3 gives you an opportunity to practice the skills you have learned so far:

- Reading and understanding a statute
- Close case reading
- Briefing a case
- Deconstructing and synthesizing case law to form a rule
- Identifying key client facts
- Structuring an office memo using all parts of a memo
- Formulating and writing an issue
- Writing an outline of the discussion section
- Organizing an analysis, including explaining the rule and applying the rule
- Writing the legal discussion of an objective interoffice memo
- Compiling facts from several documents
- Understanding hierarchy of authority in context
- Developing rules in a multi-issue case
- Writing an outline, draft, and final draft of a complete interoffice memo, including a fact section and legal discussion section

The new skills you will learn as you complete case file 3 include:

- Conducting independent research
- Applying a normative or policy analysis
- Drafting an e-mail to a client

MEMORANDUM

To: Associates
From: Supervising Attorney
Re: *Berger v. Photo Restorations, LLC*, South Dakota Personal Jurisdiction
Date: XXX

Please prepare a memo for one of our clients, Photo Restorations, LLC. The company's main office is located in Austin, Texas. Zoe Graham owns the company. Zoe specializes in restoration of vintage photos. She has several components to her business including sales, appraisals, repair and restoration. Her business is successful and she has a worldwide reputation. Photo Restorations uses the internet to facilitate business and has customers in every state.

A former Photo Restorations customer, Sally Berger, has filed a complaint in a South Dakota circuit court. Berger sent Photo Restorations three photographs for repair and restoration. She claims two of the photos were damaged in the process. Though Zoe has attempted to work things out with her, they have reached an impasse. Zoe is adamant that she performed the restoration work agreed to by contract.

I need to know whether the South Dakota court will have personal jurisdiction over Photo Restorations. Zoe's preference is not to defend the action in South Dakota because of the costs associated with litigating there. **Research, analyze, and predict whether a South Dakota state court has personal jurisdiction over Photo Restorations in this lawsuit**. Focus on the relevant South Dakota cases and the South Dakota statute relating to personal jurisdiction.

CIRCUIT COURT OF PENNINGTON COUNTY, SOUTH DAKOTA
SEVENTH JUDICIAL CIRCUIT

Sally Berger,	)	
Plaintiff,	)	
	)	COMPLAINT
v.	)	
	)	
Photo Restorations, LLC,	)	
Defendant	)	

NOW COMES the Plaintiff, Sally Berger, by and through her undersigned counsel, and complains against the Defendant as follows:

PARTIES

1. Plaintiff Sally Berger ("Berger" or "Plaintiff") is an individual residing in Rapid City, South Dakota.

2. Defendant Photo Restorations, LLC ("Photo Restorations" or "Defendant") is a limited liability corporation organized and existing under the laws of the Texas, having its principal place of business in Austin, Texas.

BACKGROUND

3. Ms. Berger inherited three photographs from her deceased husband who was a professional photographer. His photographs attracted the attention of collectors and many of his photos are now valuable.

4. The photographs have significant monetary and sentimental value to Ms. Berger. One photo entitled "Seine on Sunday" was taken on her honeymoon. The photo "Cowboy" has particular monetary value because there is a personal note written on the back to the Bergers from then President Ronald Reagan. The photo was appraised ten years ago at $7,000. The photo "Paris Lion" has an estimated value of $2,500.

5. Ms. Berger wanted to restore the photos. Over time, the photos had faded and cracked and sustained water damage.

6. In early March 2012, Ms. Berger viewed a photo restoration e-magazine titled Fotofinishing.com on the Internet. The e-magazine included feature materials about restoration of photos. While viewing the pages of this Web site, Ms. Berger opened a pop-up ad to the Web site of Defendant Photo Restorations. Defendant's Web site is named Photo4Restore.com.

7. While viewing Photo Restorations' Web site, Ms. Berger signed up to receive Photo Restorations' monthly e-newsletter via e-mail. As requested by Photo Restorations' newsletter subscription form, Ms. Berger provided personal information to Photo Restorations, such as her address and phone number.

8. Though purporting to be an e-magazine about photo restoration, Photo Restorations' newsletter Memoriesfixed.com was actually an extended advertisement and solicitation for Photo Restorations' services which included repairs to faded, torn, or damaged photos; digital restoration; or copying.

9. On approximately April 12, 2012, Photo Restorations telephoned Plaintiff at her home. The Photo Restorations representative solicited business from Plaintiff, asking her to use Photo Restorations' services.

10. During the April 12, 2012 telephone conversation, Plaintiff asked the Photo Restorations representative how much Photo Restorations charged for vintage photo repair. The Photo Restorations' representative quoted Ms. Berger a range 15 to 20 percent of the photo value.

11. On May 12, 2012, Plaintiff telephoned Photo Restorations. She expressed her interest in retaining the services of Photo Restorations, but requested that Photo Restorations provide a firm quote for restoring the photos.

12. On May 14, 2012, Photo Restorations e-mailed Plaintiff with a quote for $2,000 for restoring the photos.

13. By envelope postmarked May 15, 2012, Photo Restorations sent, via U.S. Postal Service, a written contract for the photo restoration services to Ms. Berger's residence in Rapid City, South Dakota. On May 16, 2012, Plaintiff signed one copy and mailed it from South Dakota, via U.S. Postal Service, to Photo Restorations' offices in Texas.

14. On May 20, 2012, Photo Restorations telephoned Plaintiff at her home to make shipping arrangements from South Dakota to Photo Restorations' place of business in Texas. Plaintiff expressed her interest in making her own arrangements for delivery of the photos. Due to the value of the photos, Photo Restorations then insisted that it have a local person, hired by Photo Restorations, view the photos prior to Plaintiff's delivery to Photo Restorations. Plaintiff agreed.

15. On May 29, 2012, Plaintiff sent the photos to Photo Restorations via FedEx. Several hours prior to the FedEx pickup, a local college student named Rick Brown arrived at Plaintiff's home and took pictures of the photos. Photo Restorations hired Brown to document the condition of the photos.

16. On June 1, 4, 10 and on July 3, 10, 15, 2012, the parties had telephone conversations concerning particulars of the restoration.

17. On July 30, 2012, Photo Restorations shipped the photos to Ms. Berger's home.

18. On August 1, 2012, Plaintiff wired Photo Restorations $2,000 in payment for its services.

19. On August 8, 2012, Plaintiff noticed that a section of the "Cowboy" photo had been damaged in an area that had been in perfect condition prior to May 29, 2012.

20. On August 9, 2012, Plaintiff noticed that the "Paris Lion" photo had a small tear that had not been evident prior to May 29, 2012.

21. On August 10, 2012, Plaintiff e-mailed Photo Restorations with complaints about two photos. Plaintiff demanded reimbursement of $15,000, representing the cost for repair and restoration.

22. Photo Restorations has never responded to Plaintiff's e-mail, nor to her two subsequent e-mails of August 13 and 20, 2012.

23. Photo Restorations has further never responded to Plaintiff's telephone calls placed one day after each of the e-mails on August 11, 14, and 21, 2012.

COUNT I
Breach of Contract

24. Plaintiff repeats and re-alleges the allegations of Paragraphs 1 through 20 above as if fully set forth herein.

25. Under the terms of the contract, Photo Restorations agreed to provide Ms. Berger with restored photos in exchange for Ms. Berger's agreement to pay Photo Restorations $2,000.

26. Ms. Berger has fully performed all of her obligations under the contract.

27. Photo Restorations, however, has breached the contract by failing to return fully restored photos to Ms. Berger.

28. Ms. Berger has been damaged by reason of Photo Restorations' breach.

REQUEST FOR RELIEF

WHEREFORE, the Plaintiff respectfully requests that this Court award it the following relief:

a. Compensatory, incidental, and consequential damages arising from the Defendant's breach of contract;

b. Damages in an amount equal to the fair market value of the photos in working condition;

c. Costs and prejudgment interest; and

d. Any and all further relief this Court deems to be just and proper.

Dated: October 9, 2012.

Respectfully submitted,

Kaylinn Phillip

Kaylinn Phillip, Bar No. 3322
Attorney for Plaintiff Sally Berger
One City Center
Sioux Falls, SD
555-555-1212

Dear Pat:

Thanks for reviewing Sally Berger's lawsuit against my company. I am angry about this. This is not my fault. We counseled Sally that the restoration work might need some "tweaking," but she is convinced we ruined her late dad's photos.

To tell you how well I thought the job had gone, I had hoped I would be able to feature some before and after photos of the photos on our Web site, in particular, the photo of the Seine, which we restored beautifully.

I am disappointed that this whole problem came about because we shipped the photos out in perfect shape. I am also upset that Sally just wants to blame me. You know a lawsuit is the last thing I want, but I don't want her to get away with blaming us for something we did not do.

As you requested, I am giving you my side of the story with some additional details not in her court papers. I told Sally that if she allowed us to make the arrangements for delivery that we could guarantee the condition of photos during shipping to Austin, but she refused. I think she wanted to control shipping, afraid we would make a mistake. She also said she wanted to save money and make the arrangements herself (this may have been because I would have required extensive insurance). We hired Bill, my nephew, who is a student in Rapid City, to take pictures of the photos before they were wrapped for shipping.

The photos arrived in Austin in various states of damage. We make careful notes on outbound shipping and all photos were restored to perfection. (I've attached prints of the photos, however, the damage is not visible in these copies.)

During the restoration process, in a series of phone calls, we told Sally we had difficulty repairing some of the tiny areas of damage—those only noticeable with a magnifying glass really. In the end, my best restorer made significant repairs and, as I said, the photos look great now. The sepia color that comes with age was not something that we could have (or indeed would have) tried to alter.

In all of our conversations, I told her that vintage photos are naturally going to take on some discoloring (such as the sepia discussed above) and that she should not expect a brand-new photo (which would defeat the point of restoring a vintage photo). I also specifically told her that restoration does not make a vintage photo in "good" condition turn into "mint" condition. I can't imagine Sally doesn't remember this conversation, but the lawsuit makes it seem as if she has.

What I really do not understand is why she will not let me work on the photos again. I honestly think she is trying to get $15,000 worth of restoration for $2,000. By the way, did I mention the "Cowboy" photo is probably worth around a $20,000 at auction? All of the photos are incredible. I don't think she appreciates that they are real works of art!

In addition, on August 11, 2008, I sent Sally a receipt for her check and a note telling her I would continue to work on the photos without any additional charge. Her lawsuit does not mention this at all.

Following are a few points I wanted to clarify because I think the lawsuit misstates them or at least gives a false impression of the true facts.

Our e-newsletter does provide vintage and antique photo restoration and preservation information. It also includes information about national and international photo auctions. The newsletter displays Photo Restorations' address and phone number on the front page, and has an insert box with information about our services. Photo Restorations sends the newsletter by e-mail to residents of all 50 states who have signed up for it (approximately 3,500 people/ auction houses).

During the phone conversation on May 31, Sally said to the Photo Restorations' receptionist that she had just spoken with an appraiser about the photos. The appraiser told her that vintage restoration of the photos to good condition would make them more valuable. Sally also said that the appraiser knew of my reputation and thought I would be good to the photos. Sally specifically asked us for a quote to repair and restore the photos to good condition, which as I said, for vintage photos does not mean transformation into "mint" condition.

Sally did make all the calls she claims. She was so anxious about the process. We just kept reassuring her that everything was going well, which it was.

Thanks for taking care of this, Pat. I am worried about my reputation. I am concerned that Sally will put her version of this restoration job out on the Internet and tarnish Photo Restorations' credibility.

Regards,
Zoe
Zoe Graham
Photo Restorations, LLC
125 Peach Pepper Way
Austin, Texas

Paris Lion

Seine on Sunday

Cowboy

CHAPTER 15

Applying the Skills You Have Learned

Case file 3 gives you an opportunity to practice the skills you have learned. You will likely need to go back and review some of the sections in previous chapters. Remember that this book is written as a reference for you to use in law school and after. What follows is the approach you should take as you tackle case file 3.

A. GATHERING THE FACTS

As you did with case file 2, here you will need to carefully read through the documents and make notes on the facts. The information in the memorandum, the complaint, and the letter is what you have at this point, and you should base your research and analysis on the facts therein. You will notice that the parties do not look like they agree on all the facts. You should make this clear to your reader in your fact section and you will need to account for these differences in your analysis of the problem.

> **PRACTICAL TIP**
>
> One of the documents in case file 3 is a civil complaint. As you know from civil procedure, this is the pleading that a plaintiff files with the court to initiate a lawsuit. A complaint states the cause of action and the facts supporting the cause of action. It also contains the damages requested. A complaint is sworn to by the plaintiff, so the allegations are considered truthful. However, remember that the complaint only represents one side's version. The opposing party files an answer (not included here) that responds to the plaintiff's allegations.

How do you write about facts that conflict? The best way is to alert the reader explicitly in the fact section that there are discrepancies. You do not need to mention the discrepancy in the issue or summary unless the discrepancy is the actual issue in the case.

In case file 2, assume that there had been one more police report where the officer has written down that "a large crowd including about 25 people had formed on the sidewalk outside of Mr. Matthew's house." Now you have two conflicting reports, one that says about 7 people had gathered and one that says a larger crowd of 25 had gathered. From your research you know that this is a critical fact because it is evidence about whether Matthew's conduct was "public" under the statute.

In your fact section you can show this to the reader explicitly:

> The two police reports contained in the file are not consistent as to the number of onlookers present at the scene. While Officer X reports that there were 25 people present, Officer Y wrote that there were 7 onlookers.

Notice that no attempt is made to justify, characterize, or explain the difference. You would only include a justification if it came from one of the parties in the case and was therefore part of the facts.

In your legal analysis, you may have to address how the conflict in facts could change the outcome of the case. For example, if in the Matthew case there was the discrepancy about the number of onlookers, you would have to show the reader that the number of onlookers could influence whether the court finds that Matthew's behavior rises to being "public" under the statute. For example:

> The number of onlookers who witnessed Matthew's conduct is not clear from the record. Officer X says there were 7 and Officer Y says there were 25. Evidence of the crowd size is a factor the court will consider in deciding if the conduct is "public," and the discrepancy here could lead to different conclusions. Although 7 onlookers shows that Matthew's behavior "affected the public," a court is more likely to find that behavior that draws a crowd of 25 more decisively shows that it "affected the public."

This section would be part of your application.

B. USING THE FACTS TO GENERATE SEARCH TERMS FOR RESEARCH

Because you will be doing your own research, the way to get started is to use the facts to make a list of words that you can use to find cases on point in South Dakota. If you were conducting your own research in the Matthew case, the list might look like this:

- Disorderly conduct
- Yelling
- Front porch
- Residential area
- Crowd

If you use these words to do an electronic search, the words will get you to some of the Massachusetts cases. From there you can begin reading cases and selecting the ones that look helpful. You can also use these words to find secondary sources. This is especially true for legal terms such as "disorderly conduct."

PRACTICAL TIP

Many states have "Practice Series." These are volumes written by attorneys who specialize in an area of law. For example, there is usually a Family Law Practice Series or a Criminal Law Practice Series. Many of these can be found on Westlaw and LexisNexis or are available in hard copy in a law library. These volumes are a good place to get the lay of the land concerning the area of law you are researching.

CASE FILE 3: Assignment—Review the Documents in Case File 3 and Make Notes

After reviewing and taking notes, make a list of words that you can use to generate research queries.

C. ORGANIZING CASES AND IDENTIFYING WHICH CASES TO USE

Your research will lead you to a number of cases and your task will be to narrow them down to the few that you'll need to answer the legal question. Remember to read and brief the cases that seem helpful. Study them and look for similar and distinguishable facts and rules that address when a court can exercise personal jurisdiction. You will also find a statute on point. Review Chapter 4 to remind yourself how to understand a statute. Once you have identified the cases that will guide your analysis of the problem, make an organizing chart like the one in Chapter 6. There may only be a few cases to use. Make sure any case you use is still good law and hasn't been overturned or narrowed.

D. START WRITING THE DISCUSSION SECTION

Remember the steps you go through in drafting the discussion from Chapter 8, which are reprinted below. In case file 3, the legal issue has been identified for you, so you'll start with step 2.

1. Identify the legal issue.
2. Research the law.
3. Study the law.
4. Organize the information you have read.
5. Synthesize the rule(s).

6. Make an outline of your legal analysis.
7. Write a draft of the analysis.
8. Revise the draft.
9. Revise the draft again as needed.
10. Proofread and line edit.

Once you have researched and gathered the cases you think will be helpful, organize them using a chart or some other method that is suitable to your personal style. Students often ask how to know whether they have found enough cases. One way to feel reassured that your research is complete is if the opinions keep circling back to the same core cases when they cite to the rules. Shepardizing and Keyciting carefully will also help you know that you have read all the relevant cases. Remember, this process takes quite a bit of time, especially as you are starting out.

CASE FILE 3: Assignment—Write the Rule on Personal Jurisdiction That Pertains to Your Case

After you write a draft of the rule, you are ready to draft the roadmap paragraph and an outline. You may discover holes or questions about your analysis as you draft these. The research and case studying process is ongoing during a project. Sometimes your analysis becomes clearer as you begin to draft and you need to re-read cases. That is a good thing! It shows that you are involved in an ever recursive process of finding the best answer supported by the law—all signs of careful lawyering.

From your outline, write your first draft of the memorandum's discussion section. Keep in mind that this is likely to be revised substantially, but you need to get pen to paper to get the process going. Remember to consider and address the counter-analysis.

E. WRITING A NORMATIVE OR POLICY ANALYSIS

Very often there will be a piece of your legal discussion that calls for an analysis based on reason, policy, or normative societal standards. For example, negligence standards in tort law usually turn on issues of what was reasonable under the circumstances. To identify what is reasonable, courts often look to what the current norms are. When courts are resolving issues regarding new law or deciding a case where there is a split in court decisions, they frequently include some analysis that is based on norms to show why one result makes more sense than another. The *Diaz* case on page 34 and referred to on page 67 is an example of this type of reasoning.

Assume your supervisor tells you she has a client who was arrested for shoplifting. After the arrest, the police took her cell phone, opened it, and searched it. They found photos that incriminated the client. Your supervisor wants to know if the police searched the phone illegally. In your research you discover that the courts in your state have not definitively ruled on the issue. The decisions that come close to addressing it typically apply an analysis of traditional Fourth Amendment search and seizure law, but the courts also discuss the difficulty of applying Fourth Amendment law in the age of smartphones and laptops.

In writing the memorandum to your supervisor, in addition to explaining and applying the Fourth Amendment law, you will need to explain that the courts consider current norms regarding new technology and phones. How do you do that? Unlike analogical reasoning based on precedent, normative reasoning has more of a narrative style. Here is an example of what you might say in a paragraph that would come after your application of the law:

> The defendant may be able to argue here that there is a meaningful difference between searching her iPhone and searching a wallet or purse. Although the court is likely to apply a traditional Fourth Amendment analysis, it is also likely that the court will recognize that new technologies allow for large amounts of private data to be stored on an iPhone. (Here you might cite to one of the cases that come close to your issue and use the normative analysis.) The type of information that can be stored of most relevance to law enforcement would be photographs, documents, e-mails, and written messages. With respect to those types of files, the only difference between the iPhone searched here and a laptop computer is the sheer volume of such materials that may be stored on each. If the state argues that the iPhone at issue here is merely a closed container, then warrantless laptop computer searches would also be permissible, a result that our court would probably think too far reaching.

Using a normative approach to answer a legal issue allows you to use your common sense. Though you must have a legal basis for using this type of analysis, the basis usually comes from cases where the court applied a normative analysis. Remember, judges are people and they make decisions based on several things, including what makes sense. Courts are interested in keeping up with the times and refraining from illogical decisions. They are also interested in being fair and just. It will rarely be the case that you rely solely on a normative analysis. Usually, this piece of the analysis will be one paragraph or short section of an analysis that is otherwise based on cases and statutes.

F. REVISIONS

The first draft is just that. The final product may look very different. The revision stage may take almost as long as it took to research and write the first draft. Once you have a solid draft, consider using a checklist to help you edit further. Here is one checklist, but you may also develop your own.

Issue
☐ Include decisive facts and legal points.

Summary (or Brief Answer)
☐ Start with a quick answer.
☐ Give the overall rule and apply it to the client's problem.
☐ Don't include cites.
☐ Limit to one paragraph.

Facts
☐ Include facts for context.
☐ Use an objective tone.
☐ Include decisive facts.
☐ Include all facts in the discussion section of the memorandum.
☐ Include both adverse and helpful facts for your client.
☐ Do not include legal citations.
☐ Include procedural history of client's case, if relevant.
☐ Tell a story that is logical and makes sense.

Roadmap Paragraph (looks very similar to the summary, but it includes cites and does not apply the client's problem to the rule)
☐ In the first sentence, give the conclusion on the issue that applies the rule to the facts.
☐ State the overall statute/rule/test(s).
☐ Alert the reader to any givens or issues you are not going to address.
☐ Include policy IF it is relevant to the overall rule.

Explanation of the Law
☐ Each paragraph should begin with a specific conclusion sentence or two that shows the reader the reasons for your prediction.
☐ Organize the paragraphs around principles from the rule using topic or thesis sentences (and words) that alert the reader to which part of the rule you are explaining.
☐ Follow the same sequence and organization as the explanation paragraphs.
☐ Give brief examples from cases, if appropriate.

Application of the Law to Client's Problem
☐ Begin with a conclusion sentence that tells the reader where you are going.
☐ Show the reader how the rules apply to your client's facts using similar language.
☐ Apply the rules or reasoning of the precedent to illustrate why your analogies or distinctions are significant and why the court will likely rule in line with your argument.

☐ Use clear sentence structure, concrete nouns and verbs, and transitions to communicate precisely and efficiently.

☐ The comparisons should be obvious and significant.

☐ The comparisons should refer to (not restate) decisive facts.

☐ The comparisons should include reasoning (why the comparison matters).

Counter-Analysis

☐ Use words or phrases that alert the reader you are shifting to the counter-analysis.

☐ Give the specific alternative analysis.

☐ Show how the law might support the alternative analysis.

☐ Refute the counter-analysis.

Appendix

To: Professor
From: Student
Date: November 8, XXXX
Re: Molly Jackson Negligence Action

Issue

Under Texas law, which holds a minor to a lesser standard of care than an adult, was Molly Jackson, a mentally challenged 14-year-old, contributorily negligent when she was struck by Susan Green's car as she walked to her school bus stop wearing dark clothing and without a light?

Summary

Probably not. Texas courts measure a minor's standard of care by comparing it to the care that a child of the same age, intelligence, experience, and capacity would use. For a court to hold Molly contributorily negligent, it would have to find that she failed to meet this standard of care. Because of her mental challenges, a court would evaluate Molly by the standard of an ordinary 10-year-old and determine that a child of this age could not have foreseen the danger posed by the weather and road conditions. Thus, the court would likely find that Molly's failure to wear bright clothing or carry a light was reasonable and not contributorily negligent given her developmental age.

Fact

Our client, Molly Jackson, suffered serious injury after a car driven by Susan Green hit her as she walked to her bus stop. Molly is a 14-year-old girl who is mentally and behaviorally four years behind others her age. Molly wants to sue Green for negligence. We must determine if Green is likely to succeed with an affirmative defense of contributory negligence.

Molly lives with her family near the bottom of Wagon Hill Road in Brownville. Molly's morning trip to the school bus had followed the same route every day for the prior three years. Molly would walk down her driveway and turn right. She would stay on the right-hand side of the road until she got to the top of the hill. At the top, she would check for traffic in both directions, cross to the left side of the street, and walk the rest of the way to her bus stop.

Last December 6, just after her 14th birthday, Molly left the house to go to the school bus as usual. She had not quite gotten to the top of the hill when Green's car hit her. It was early morning, dark, and the road was snow covered with snow banks along the shoulders. There were no sidewalks. Molly was wearing dark clothing and was not carrying a light.

Green was driving in the same direction on Wagon Hill Road at a modest speed. As another vehicle approached, Green dimmed her headlights. When she re-engaged her bright lights, she saw Molly in the road. Green hit Molly, causing her to suffer numerous internal injuries and several broken bones.

Discussion

A judge would probably not find Molly contributorily negligent because she acted with due care under the minor standard. A child between ages 5 and 14 may be contributorily negligent if the child failed to use such care as an ordinarily prudent child of the same age, intelligence, experience, and capacity would have exercised under the same or similar circumstances. *Rudes v. Gottschalk*, 324 S.W.2d 201, 206 (Tex. 1959); *MacConnell v. Hill*, 569 S.W.2d 524, 527 (Tex. App. 1978); *City of Austin v. Hoffman*, 379 S.W.2d 103, 107 (Tex. App. 1964); *Dallas Ry. & Terminal Co. v. Rogers*, 218 S.W.2d 456, 458 (Tex. 1949). A child's developmental capacity is relevant in assessing the correct standard of care to apply. *Soledad v. Lara*, 762 S.W.2d 212, 214 (Tex. App. 1988). Texas courts are reluctant to hold children responsible even if they failed to keep a proper lookout or heed warnings. *MacConnell*, 569 S.W.2d at 527. The test of negligence is different for children than for adults because the powers and abilities of children to anticipate danger and harmful consequences are often not the same as adults. *Rudes*, 324 S.W.2d at 206.

The standard of care applied to a child is measured by the behavior that would be reasonable under the circumstances given the child's particular abilities. *Houston & T.C.R. Co. v. Bulger*, 80 S.W. 557, 561 (Tex. App. 1904); *Soledad v. Lara*, 762 S.W.2d 212, 214 (Tex. App. 1988). In *Bulger*, a 13-year-old boy with a low mental capacity scalded both legs when hot water and steam escaped from a boiler at a railroad company's pumping station. *80 S.W. at 561*. The court upheld the lower court's jury charge to consider the boy's low mental capacity, holding that the boy may not have had the same discretion that could reasonably be expected from other 13-year-old children. *Id.* Similarly, in *Soledad*, a 16-year old boy sued the design engineers of a drainage ditch where he was injured while playing. 762 S.W.2d at 214. The boy sued under the attractive nuisance doctrine and the court held that even though ordinarily the attractive nuisance doctrine does not apply to children over 14, it did apply in Soledad's case because the boy was lacking in mental development, as evidenced by his attendance in special education classes. *Id.*

Texas courts are reluctant to find children contributorily negligent where they have failed to keep a proper lookout for their own safety or to heed warnings. *See Guzman v. Guajardo*, 761 S.W.2d 506, 510 (Tex. App. 1988); *MacConnell*, 569 S.W.2d at 527. In *Guzman*, a seven-year-old boy was hit and killed by a car as he crossed a road. 761 S.W.2d at 510. The court upheld the lower court's decision that the boy was not contributorily negligent even though he was warned by his mother and grandmother specifically to stay off that particular road earlier that day. *Id*. Similarly, in *MacConnell*, a six-year-old boy was sprayed with hot steam and water when the defendant negligently removed the end of a car's radiator hose without first properly releasing the pressure. 569 S.W.2d at 525. The defendant had warned the boy twice to move away from the car. *Id*. The court reversed the lower court's jury decision that found the boy contributorily negligent, noting that the boy's failure to keep a proper lookout was not enough to bar his recovery because of his inferior ability to foresee and anticipate danger. *Id* at 528.

The experience and education of a child in the injury-causing activity does not necessarily make a child contributorily negligent. *Dallas Ry. & Terminal Co.*, 218 S.W.2d at 461; *Guzman*, 761 S.W.2d at 510. In *Dallas Ry. & Terminal Co.*, an 11-year-old girl familiar with the traffic hazards of downtown Dallas was hit by a bus as she crossed an intersection. 218 S.W.2d at 461. Reversing the jury's findings that the girl was contributorily negligent for failing to keep a proper lookout, the court held that even if a child has been instructed and is experienced in traffic matters, a higher standard of care should not be applied because the child is still subject to the reckless and impulsive nature of youth. *Id*. Similarly, the boy in *Guzman* was educated by his mother in traffic matters and was taught the importance of keeping a lookout for cars. *Guzman*, 761 S.W.2d at 510. The boy's traffic education did not affect the court's decision against finding him contributorily negligent. *Id*.

In evaluating Molly's potential contributory negligence, a court would first look at her age and mental capacity. Like the minors in *Bulger* and *Soledad*, who both showed signs of mental challenges, here testing has revealed that Molly is mentally and behaviorally four years behind other children her age. Although Molly was 14 years old at the time of the accident, the court will likely apply the standard of care of a ten-year-old child. Moreover, as in *Bulger*, where the court instructed the jury to consider that the child may not have had the same discretion that could be reasonably expected from other children of the same age, here the court is likely to give a jury the same instruction regarding Molly's developmental age.

A court would also probably determine that Molly, at her age and mental capacity, could not have foreseen the danger surrounding the circumstances on the day of the accident. Unlike *Guzman*, where the child's mother had instructed him in traffic safety, our facts do not indicate that Molly was warned about the hazards of walking to the bus stop on a dark, snowy street. Even if Molly had been warned of the danger on her road, it is unlikely that this would affect the court's decision in her favor given that in *Guzman* the warnings made no difference to the standard of care.

A court may determine that Molly's neglect to wear reflective clothing and to carry a light was a failure to keep a proper lookout for her safety. However, like the boy in *MacConnell*, Molly's inferior ability to anticipate danger as a minor should protect her from being held contributorily negligent. Her case may even be stronger than *MacConnell* because, arguably, she kept a proper lookout by walking on the right side of the street to the top of the hill until she could safely cross, thus avoiding the problem of non-visible oncoming traffic.

Molly's experience walking the same route for three years does not make it more likely that a court will find her contributorily negligent. Like the girl in *Dallas Ry. & Terminal Co.*, Molly was experienced in the everyday hazards presented by her route. Her manner of walking to the top of the hill before crossing the street is evidence that she was aware of traffic dangers. However, the girl's experience with traffic in *Dallas Ry. & Terminal Co.* did not make her contributorily negligent because her relative youth still could have lowered her ability to judge the circumstances. Similarly, Molly's experience with traffic should not increase the chance that a court will find her contributorily negligent.

Conclusion

A court will probably take into consideration Molly's ten-year-old mental capacity. Any evidence of Molly's experience in traffic matters, or her failure to keep a proper lookout or to heed warnings, is unlikely to result in a finding that permits Green to raise the affirmative defense of contributory negligence.

Index

CPSIA information can be obtained
at www.ICGtesting.com
Printed in the USA
LVHW101110100620
657786LV00002B/243